COMPETITIVENESS AND CORPORATE CULTURE

T0358514

Competitiveness and Corporate Culture

HIDEO YAMASHITA

Routledge
Taylor & Francis Group

LONDON AND NEW YORK

First published 1998 by Ashgate Publishing

Reissued 2018 by Routledge
2 Park Square, Milton Park, Abingdon, Oxon, OX14 4RN
711 Third Avenue, New York, NY 10017

Routledge is an imprint of the Taylor & Francis Group, an informa business

Copyright © Hideo Yamashita 1998

All rights reserved. No part of this book may be reprinted or reproduced or utilised in any form or by any electronic, mechanical, or other means, now known or hereafter invented, including photocopying and recording, or in any information storage or retrieval system, without permission in writing from the publishers.

Notice:
Product or corporate names may be trademarks or registered trademarks, and are used only for identification and explanation without intent to infringe.

Publisher's Note
The publisher has gone to great lengths to ensure the quality of this reprint but points out that some imperfections in the original copies may be apparent.

Disclaimer
The publisher has made every effort to trace copyright holders and welcomes correspondence from those they have been unable to contact.

A Library of Congress record exists under LC control number: 98072961

ISBN 13: 978-1-138-61622-6 (hbk)
ISBN 13: 978-0-429-46235-1 (ebk)

Contents

Figures and tables

Acknowledgements

I would like to express my sincere appreciation to Tan Chwee Huat, Professor, former Dean, Faculty of Business Administration, National University of Singapore, for his support and endorsement of this book. I am extremely grateful for the support and encouragement given to me by Jon A. Turner, Professor, Stern School of Business, New York University. I greatly appreciate the much-needed, useful and valuable review that Ikujiro Nonaka, Professor, Institute of Innovation Research, Hitotsubashi University, has provided me with. I also wish to thank Michael Scott Morton, Professor, Sloan School of Management, MIT, for giving me insightful comments and valuable suggestions. In addition, I am especially grateful for the review and thoughtful comments that Michael Beer, Professor Harvard Business School, has given to me. Tan Thiam Soon, former Vice Dean, Faculty of Business Administration, National University of Singapore, has provided sustained support and encouragement to me over the years. Shandon Alderson, my colleague, was of great assistance in finalizing the chapters. I also extend my thanks to Sarah Markham, Kate Hargreave and other editorial staff at Ashgate. Finally, thanks to Makoto Iida, Founder of Secom Group, to whom I owe so much.

Whatever the weaknesses of this book, they are mine alone.

Preface

Competitiveness and corporate culture. Competitiveness is something we have to deal with throughout our lives. Whether it is visible or invisible, it is always with us. Corporate culture, on the other hand, seems to be set before us. It looks to be already prepared. The truth is, however, that corporate culture is what we make, form, and support. Since it takes a long time to build and changes slowly, corporate culture seems to be given to us.

Enterprise competitiveness is the competitiveness of a firm. Both managers and staff form and support a structure of enterprise competitiveness. In addition, they hold their national culture in the form of views, ways of thinking and state of being. Corporate culture is, on the other hand, the personality of a firm. What makes up its personality is the cultural elements ascribed to the members of a firm. The combination of cultural elements and their strength and weakness differ from one company to another. It is these differences, to put it precisely, which form a firm's corporate culture. Corporate culture changes with time. Thus, the firm's structure of competitiveness, in which its corporate culture is duly reflected, changes as well. If that change is in the right direction, it is to be encouraged. If not, it is to be stopped and turned around.

This book starts with the subject of competitiveness which is put in perspective of national culture. The competitiveness of a state is affiliated with its culture. How they are affiliated is, then, the first subject to address and a necessary step to get to the theme of enterprise competitiveness and its corporate culture. The cultures we take up and explain here are Japanese and US cultures. Therefore, such questions as the following are asked. What is Japanese culture ? What attributes can be found in it ? How are those attributes related to competitiveness ? On the other hand, what is the US culture ? What attributes can be recognized in it ? What relationships do they have with competitiveness ? These are the topics in the first half of the book. Then, in the second half, the following items are discussed. What is a healthy Japanese corporate culture? What is an unhealthy Japanese corporate culture? How do they positively or negatively affect competitiveness? How does a healthy corporate culture turn into an unhealthy one or vice versa? On the other hand, what is a healthy US corporate culture? What is an unhealthy US corporate culture? How does each of one positively or negatively affect competitiveness? How does a good corporate culture change into a bad one or vice versa? And finally, with a case of Danish concern, we shall see how an unhealthy corporate culture turns into a healthy one sufficient to strengthen its competitiveness.

There are other competitiveness-enhancing factors than corporate culture. Among the elements constituting a competitiveness structure, technology is certainly one of the essential ingredients. Information technology is particularly significant in that respect. Advancement and development in information technology have been remarkable in the recent years. New and innovative ideas have appeared almost every three months in the IT field. The reengineering thought, in this context, has been publicized widely as an advocate of IT technology. We have to face the reality, however, that more than 70 % of reengineering attempts have failed. In cases that succeeded, moreover, the people in charge of changing the organization did not follow the way implied in the literature, but took on a much broader approach. As will be explained later, there seems to be some contradictions in logic of the reengineering theories.

A firm is an organization of individuals who have their own modes of viewing, ways of thinking and state of being. If one talks about a firm's competitiveness leaving aside its corporate culture, it is like discussing a living being and neglecting its vital organs. The firm is a living being and has its own personality.

1   What is competitiveness ?

Competitiveness covers the state economy (i.e., the macro-economy) and the enterprise (i.e., the micro-economy). Then, when we say that a state economy is competitive, or that an enterprise is competitive, how is that competitiveness demonstrated ? Competitiveness does not imply comparative predominance attained through short-term speculation, dumping, unjust dealings, market overprotection, and the like. It does not mean attempting to make a profit by monopoly or unfair practices either. Competitiveness represents attempting to hold long-term, stable predominance in a just and free market economy. Accordingly, the foundation of competitiveness is, in the first place, the social ethos to promote independence, to pursue fairness, and to regard stoicism as a value. Following social ethos are the development and promotion of a free market (trade) system, a provision of a legal foundation, an education system, and the establishment of ethics, which derive from, and uphold the social ethos. We will call these myriad concepts 'Social Logistics' (in short, Logistics here).

Logistics are necessary as, so to speak, circumstantial conditions. They do not represent competitiveness per se for actors involved in competition. A state or a firm has to prepare an economic base on its own. This base is generally named the infrastructure which is divided into two groups : physical assets (facilities, machinery, networks, etc.) and human resources (entrepreneurs, scientists, engineers, skilled workers, etc.). Next, significant and effective investment has to be made incessantly for a state or a firm to develop continuously. Therefore, the investment base has to be built up. Furthermore, environmental improvement and conservation is indispensable for investment and growth to circulate favorably without intervention. Environmental impediments will retard the circulation of investment, and limit growth. Those impediments are significant hurdles to overcome for social progress to continue. As the final element of this base, we must consider the diffusion of ideas and planning. New inventions, original planning, novel ideas, and the like come into effect

1

only when they are diffused to their related industries or related departments. The mechanism and the speed of diffusion become a requisite for effectiveness. Much of the meaning of telecommunications today can be found here. Taken together, we will call these requisites for actors involved in competition the 'Economic Base'.

Now that Logistics and the Economic Base are set, competitiveness enters the active arena for performers. It is effectiveness that is the first focal point for either a state's activities or a firm's activities. There are many things to do in attaining effectiveness, such as how to commercialize technology, how to improve cost, quality, and delivery terms, how to make use of communication, how to abolish competition restrictive practices, and so on. Next, it is ethics, that form a significant set of elements. In this category, there are diligence, pride, morals, relations between management and workers, and the like. In real economic activities, however, there are quite a few instances where there is no alternative but to select a balance between effectivity and ethics. For example, employee education and a long-term employment guarantee are based on the trade-off between effectiveness and ethics. When we try to build industries without ethics, it will impair workers' perceptions of the work, and thus reduce the level of effectiveness in the long term. It is in this sense that the balance of effectiveness and ethics is significant, or more precisely, the tense balance is of utmost consequence. By the word 'tense', it is meant that any decision-making in this context is not to be allowed to deteriorate into a bad compromise.

All together, we will call this arena for actors above the 'Management System'. To sum up, competitiveness is composed of three layers : Logistics, Economic Base, and Management System. We will term this 'the Three-Layer Structure of Competitiveness', outlined in the following figure. The elements of competitiveness are, in turn, shown in Table 1.1.

2

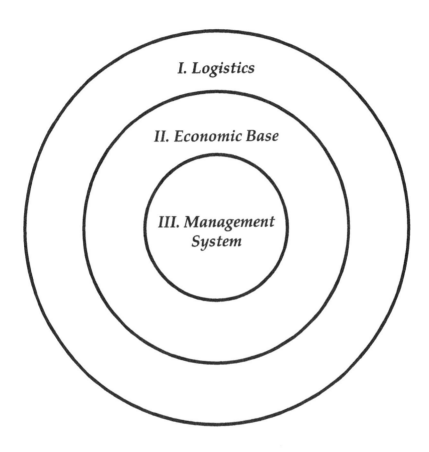

Figure 1.1 Three-Layer Structure of Competitiveness

Table 1.1   Elements of competitiveness

I   Logistics

- Social ethos
  Promoting independence
  Pursuing fairness
  Valuing stoicism
- Upkeep and promotion of free market (trade) system
- Legal foundation
- Education
- Ethics

II   Economic Base

- Infrastructure

Physical assets	Facilities, machinery, network
Human resources	Entrepreneurs, scientists, engineers, skilled workers

- Build-up of investment foundation
- Environment improvement and conservation
- Diffusion of new ideas, planning and others

III Management System

A. Effectiveness
- Improving cost, quality and delivery terms
- Freely and openly introducing and developing new technologies and systems
- Abolishing competition-restrictive practices
- Activating communication
- Encouraging competitive spirit

B. Tense balance between effectiveness and ethics
- Organizing techniques
- Organization where workers have little consciousness of organizational hierarchy
- Encouraging initiative
- Using flexible methods that can meet any situation
- Decision-making processes with a variety of alternatives
- Opportunity for continual education and training

4

C. Ethics
- View of purity
- Fair practices
- Diligence
- Workers as leading actors
- Pride and self-confidence in work
- Ethics of management-worker relations

The Three-Layer Structure of Competitiveness

The first layer, the outermost layer, is Logistics, and surrounds the second and third layers. The second layer is the Economic Base. The third layer is the Management System which is at the core of the Three-Layer Structure of Competitiveness. The Economic Base supports the Management System as the arena for acting performers, and thus encircles the third layer. The Three-Layer Structure forms the competitiveness of a state or of an enterprise. Now that we have come up with the Three-Layer Structure of Competitiveness, how is, then, competitiveness generally argued ? What social and economic elements are considered to be significant in strengthening competitiveness ? To elaborate further on this point, we will refer to some leading sources on competitiveness in regard to the elements of the Three-Layer Structure of Competitiveness.

The Council on Competitiveness, founded in 1986, is a nonprofit, nonpartisan organization of chief executives from business, higher education and organized labor who have joined together to pursue a single overriding goal : to improve the ability of American companies and workers to compete more effectively in world markets. Their views on competitiveness are summarized briefly in the Recommendations, Chapter IV of the *Gaining New Ground* published in 1989. Among their views,

1   Assessment of how federal laws, economic policies and guidelines affect the time horizons of US managers.
(This apparently relates to Legal Foundation of Logistics, The Three-Layer Structure of Competitiveness.)
2   Orient federal laws and regulations to the reality of the international market place and strengthen the performance of the key agencies.
(This relates, again, to Legal Foundation of Logistics.)
3   Create a US economic climate more conducive to manu-facturing, innovation and investment in technology.
(This is concerned with Social Ethos of Logistics.)

4 Macro-economic actions that reduce the budget deficit and increase national savings.
(This is related to Build-Up of Investment Foundation of Economic Base.)

5 Make the R&D tax credit permanent and amend it to include manufacturing engineering and process R&D.
(It has bearing on Build-Up of Investment Foundation of Economic Base.)

6 Promote supplier networks that cooperate to set standards and share information in critical technologies.
(It relates to Diffusion of New Ideas, Planning and Others of Economic Base.)

7 Develop policies and programs to ensure that America has a world-class technology infrastructure.
(It is concerned with Infrastructure of Economic Base.)

8 Establish more effective networks among US industry groups to accelerate the diffusion of technology, facilitate commercialization and promote leadership in critical generic technologies.
(It relates to Diffusion of New Ideas, Planning and Others of Economic Base.)

9 Improve ability to reach out and bring technology to market rapidly in the form of quality products, processes and services.
(It is concerned with Commercializing Technology of A. Effectiveness, Management System.)

10 Institute total quality management and continuous improvement.
(It is concerned with Improving Cost, Quality and Delivery Terms of A. Effectiveness, Management System.)

11 US firms should motivate, train and empower their employees to take responsibility for achieving their goals.
(It relates to Encouraging Initiative of B. Tense Balance between Effectiveness and Ethics, Management System.)

12 Employees at all levels of industry should be involved in the effort to improve technological competitiveness.
(It has bearing on Diligence and Workers as Leading Actors of C. Ethics, Management System.)

13 Continuously upgrade the skills of the work force.
(It relates to Opportunity for Continual Education and Training of B. Tense Balance between Effectiveness and Ethics, Management System.)

14 Make efforts, in cooperation with employees, to ensure that educational programs in engineering and management reflect the real needs of the manufacturing and service sectors.
(It has bearing, again, on Opportunity for Continual Education and Training of B. Tense Balance between Effectiveness and Ethics, Management System.)

As shown above, the views of the Council fit well with the elements of the Three-Layer Structure of Competitiveness. Although the Council makes such recommendations to remedy the situation in the US, they are applicable, as well, to any country facing issues of competitiveness.
    As for Education of Logistics, we can refer to *America in the Global '90s* by A. H. Kiplinger and K. A. Kiplinger. They say, 'For business people, lending a hand to local schools is no longer just a civic duty.... It's a matter of self-interest, perhaps even self-preservation.... There's growing recognition that schools are everybody's responsibility, and that money alone won't fix the system'. (Ibid. P 155 and P 162)   They further argue, 'Today we have come to see that the business of America is education, and quality education is inseparable from achievement in the market place...As a result, we are more interested in US educational policies than in US export policies'. (Ibid. P 155 and P 162)
    Furthermore, we will refer to *Global Competitiveness* edited by Martin K. Starr. As to the legal system, 'US international competitiveness is affected by its litigiousness...the greatest on earth. Japan trains 1,000 engineers for every 100 lawyers ; the United States trains 1,000 lawyers for every 100 engineers'. (Ibid. P 17)   The legal system has, thus, much bearing on Infrastructure (Human Resources) of Economic Base as well as Legal Foundation of Logistics.   As for the openness of the US market, it says, 'In reality, the US market is not that open. The small nation of Singapore, for example, has a more open environment than does the United States. Virtually every form of regulation confronted by US firms in foreign countries also exists in the United State'. (Ibid. P 256)   The above remark is concerned with Upkeep and Promotion of Free Market (Trade) System of Logistics. It further argues, 'McDonald's success abroad has been attributed to exporting not only food but management skills as well...The company uses a tight-loose management style that tightly controls operating procedures but allows a loose approach to individual creativity'. (Ibid. P 267)   The argument above has relevance to A. Effectiveness and Encouraging initiative of B. Tense balance between effectiveness and ethics, Management System. It is pointed out, moreover, that 'Attitudes, social organization and moral value : these underlie and

7

explain America's industrial achievement'. (Ibid. P 74)   This remark is concerned with Social ethos and Ethics of Logistics. It insists, in this connection, that 'productivity and creative contribution of a worker to the production process depend on the extent to which workers feel they have a stake in their work, and that they are valued members of economic community'. (Ibid. P 92)   This insistence relates to Pride and self-confidence in work and Ethics of management-worker relations of C. Ethics, Management System.

As has been seen, the leading sources on competitiveness have the same connotations in their remarks as the Three-Layer Structure of Competitiveness. It seems, therefore, that the Competitiveness Model can be applied extensively.

2   What is culture ?

Now, we shall move into the second subject of the book, culture.

2.1 Culture in general

What is culture ?   We can cite, as examples, traditional dramas, dances and songs, buildings aged several centuries, paintings of the past, and so forth. They are things of culture, and called the 'overt culture' since they are explicit in existence. One can see them whenever he or she visits a nation.

On the other hand, there is culture that one can not necessarily see although he or she has been in its place or lived his or her life for quite a time there. This is called the 'covert culture', and can not be easily understood unless a person is keenly culture-conscious or willing to learn it. As an example, T. Suzuki takes a British way of thinking on horses.

> It seems that British people see horses as man's friend just as they do dogs. It is abhorrent for them to hear that someone eats horseflesh. Eating horsemeat would sound almost like cannibalism. If a Japanese asks for some horsemeat at a butcher's shop, therefore, the British would see him having a queer eating habit, or, to the extreme, see Japanese people as a whole being a cruel human race. Feelings toward horses are utterly different between the British and the Japanese although there is little difference found in the use and roles expected of them in real life between both peoples. I have tried to ask those who visited Britain as a traveler or stayed there for a long time how the British think horseflesh. No one expressed, however, such a view above. I have recognized again the difficulties for people to take notice of a covert culture in a foreign country. (T Suzuki, 1973)

When we say 'culture', therefore, there are two kinds. One is the overt culture which is viewable and discernible, and the other is the covert culture which is difficult to see and likely to be unnoticed.

Culture is made, formed, and supported by people of a nation, whether it is overt or covert. What would, then, drive people to make, form, and support it ? It is not things of instinct nor inbred in nature. It is the second womb and nurtured through learning at home and in the community following one's birth. (Ryotaro Shiba, 1989) It is an accumulation of modes of viewing things, ways of thinking and state of being which are characteristic of a nation's people. Here is the essence of culture. That is, 'culture' is a frame or structure in ways of thought and deed specific to a group of people which is handed down through learning from their ancestors to descendants, from their parents to children. (T. Suzuki, 1973)

To be noted here is that culture can be learned. Culture differs from nation to nation, but every culture is learnable. Since it can be learned, we can master and meet with other cultures just as well. That is pretty good news, in particular, for international business. (Gary P. Ferraro, 1990)

Culture is not a thing distanced from us. It is the accumulation of modes of viewing, ways of thinking and state of being which go with our daily life. Keita Asari, a stage director, has this to say : 'Modern Japanese life is more analogous to a Japanese version of modern English drama than Noh or Kabuki'. Culture changes all the time, but it also embraces the things inherited from time immemorial.

3   Japanese culture

When people speak of the Japanese culture, there are generally three different lines of thought. One is the Kami Way which is, in the author's view, not a religion, but an accumulation of human intelligence. The second is Confucianism and the third is Buddhism, both of which were originally brought in from overseas. Out of the above, Buddhism is now recognized only to be instrumental in performing a funeral ceremony. It is rather removed from the essence of culture since, today, it has little to do with the modes of viewing things, ways of thinking and state of being of Japanese people which are duly reflected in their daily life. That leaves the Kami Way and Confucianism for our discussion. Which is truly the leading culture, then ?

Since the publication of *The Chrysanthemum and the Sword* by Ruth Benedict, most scholars have tried to interpret and explain Japanese culture through Confucianist mentality. That trend has been further promoted by Chie Nakane whose thoughts are expressed in her book, *Japanese Society.*   Not a few scholars, moreover, insist that the greater part of Japanese heritage was nurtured during the period of Tokugawa shogunate (1603-1867) when the country was, as a rule, closed to outside in trade and other interchange. During that period, the government is said to have taken the basic policy of ruling the country by Confucianist thought. Modern Japanese people are, they argue, firmly guided by such Confucianist heritage in their thought and deed.

Now, is it really so ?   Is their argument convincing enough for the most Japanese to accept ?   The author's answer is 'No'.

In the first place, the Tokugawa shogunate was not a power-centered government. It was not dictatorial, but a coalition government in essence. Its policies could not possibly have pervaded all the lords' domains in the country.

In the second place, those scholars above often argue that the society of the Tokugawa age was virtual in structure. In other words, they think that people were more conscious of a ruler-subordinate relationship

11

than a community-wise collegial relationship. However, the society was more flat and flexible in structure. K. Higuchi asserts,

> The vertically structured relationship can be found between master and disciple, boss and follower, warlord and retainer, parent and child, and shopkeeper and employee. On the other hand, we could also recognize that samurai warriors associated themselves with other warriors to help each other, farmers united among themselves providing mutual assistance, craftsmen related to other craftsmen in work and others, and merchants assisted each other in their business and life. Collegial cooperation was the fact of life. Accordingly, we could understand well, if we see it consisting of four layers of different classes of work upon which the administrative structure rested. (K. Higuchi, 1988)

In those days, many organizations developed autonomously among people over which the government could not actually exercise control. The administrative structure of the government, in fact, could not have worked well without those organizations. The society may well be said to have been dual in structure. (Ibid.)

In the third place, one can cite various systems of mutual assistance developed among the public which was characteristic of the Tokugawa period.

> It was in the early 19th century that Sontoku Ninomiya, a famous ardent farmer in the lordship of Odawara, invented a credit union... He came up with a system that people put out their money to help rebuilding the finance of Odawara lordship in a form of enterprise partnership or a form of syndicate finance... The system, however, was not that of his original idea. The 'Mujin-Ko', a union of mutual savings, which had already been developed among farmers, had been widely disseminated among the public. What he created was to align the Mujin-Ko in an orderly manner. (Ibid.)

People, thus, developed a system of mutual finance in their own way sufficient to meet the requirements of a lordship's economy. The society was, in that respect, much more free, open, and flexible than what the scholars, who have unduly emphasized Confucian thought at that time, would imagine.

In the fourth place, Norinaga Motoori, a scholar in those days, critiqued Confucianism as embracing a firm ruler-subordinate relationship in its moral codes. He further condemned Confucian thought because it sees heaven being against man or nature being opposed to man. He, instead, thought that man is part of nature, and nature is inside of man. Human mind, naturally, corresponds to the principles of nature. There is no ruler-subordinate relationship between deities and men, no such affiliation between nature and human beings. His argument above is natural enough for most Japanese people to accept. It is the view inherited from pre-Confucian time to the present.

Finally, one can take up the *Hagakure,* an ethics book in the Tokugawa period. The book was officially written in 1716 for samurai warriors where the ways and manners of homosexuality were written. Homosexuals were, thus, permitted in public during Tokugawa's times. In this context,

> Chinese people are curbed in thought and deed by Confucianism as European and American people are influenced by the Bible. The utmost value in Confucianism is the filial piety. It is extended to include the prayer and rites of ancestors. Accordingly, giving birth to children to keep one's life on is a must in life. Gays are sterile, cutting a string of descendants. Homosexuality, therefore, is not permitted by any means in Confucianism. (R. Shiba, 1989)

For the reasons above and others, Confucianism may well not be the main line of Japanese culture. It may only be a side line.

Things autonomous, free, open, flexible and flat are characteristic of the Kami Way. It originated in the Jomon period (from about 8000 B.C. to about 200 B.C.) and grew vigorously on the basis of a rice crop agricultural society that began in the Yayoi period (from about 200 B.C. to 200 A.D.). There is neither propagation nor missionary work in the Kami Way. It has settled deep in the Japanese mind and has become an inherent and latent culture among the Japanese. Buddhism and Confucianism were brought in from overseas when the Kami Way was already on the way to full development, and they were gradually subsumed within the Kami Way's mental framework. It represents the rhythm of life for Japanese people and encompasses all phases of communal life.

The Kami Way is the leading culture in Japan.

3.1 Characteristic attributes of the Kami Way

We shall here take up and briefly explain the most distinctive attributes of the Kami Way. As was already stated, the Kami Way has forged the Japanese mentality. But, we ought not miss the fact that the Japanese mentality, in its turn, has forged the Kami Way. People's modes of viewing, ways of thinking and state of being active in their life are the crux of culture. The following attributes are to be understood in that context, although the words or expressions of those attributes below may sound somewhat foreign.

The Musubi

Musubi implies 'giving birth' and 'making and forming'. It indicates the capacity of producing, generating, and uniting. It has a propensity to prefer production and demonstrates the high prestige of labor, taking long-range views and exerting strenuous efforts.

The Akaki-Kokoro

Akaki-Kokoro stands for 'sincerity' and 'a true heart'. To set a high value on a bright and clear mind forms an ethical basis of the Kami Way. The Akaki-Kokoro represents purity of mind. It indicates integrity and stainlessness. Cleanliness and a sense of cleanness are highly valued here.

The Misogi

Misogi (purification-making) is a spiritual exercise for people to purify themselves. In practicing Misogi, people step in an icy cold river to put the whole body in it or stand under a waterfall so that they can purify themselves, freeing them from various dirts of human egotism. Misogi represents the ethical view that purity is of the highest value. The mind of Misogi avoids Kegare (impurity), esteems cleanness, and praises youthful lives.

The Mitama-Furi

Mitama-Furi (soul-invigorating) is a spiritual exercise, similar to Misogi, conducted in the Kami Way. It is an exercise to invigorate one's exhausted and waning soul and to revive life spirits. It is, also, an exercise to introduce into one's soul a clean, bright, and right working of a deity soul. One of the typical Mitama-Furi cases is carrying a portable shrine. In a shrine festival, people carry a portable shrine on their shoulders, which is an incantatory act for Mitama-Furi.

The Hajio-Shiru-Kokoro

Hajio-Shiru-Kokoro, literally 'the shame-sensitive mind', rests upon a Japanese aesthetic view of the world attributed to their own views on cleanness and life. It is briefly comprehended in such expressions as 'Come to yourself' ; 'The Heaven knows, the Earth knows, One knows' ; 'The Heaven sees everything'.

The Kotodama

Kotodama, literally 'the spirit of words', is sent out as a message, to heighten a sense of crisis, inward to the community of its sender. Being linked with a group, a community, an assembly or the like, the power of Kotodama is expressed throughout. On the other hand, the Kotodama is sent out from one community to another to convey some important information. It is tacitly implied, here, that new ideas, ways of thinking, planning and the like are to be transferred to and propagated throughout a designated community.

The Matsuri

Matsuri originated in the plan of how to bring out the Heaven-Shining-Great-August Deity from the Heavenly Rock-Dwelling. This was planned in a divine assembly of deities in the bed of the Tranquil River of Heaven. (The Kojiki) The Matsuri is, in other words, an effort to exert an organized capacity effectively based on an assembly where members exchange ideas and plans freely, and thus enhance communication among themselves. Matsuri rituals are now carried out in a shrine. Their main purpose is to attain harmony among community residents through a community deity. The shrine also serves as an assembly hall, a public hall, a disco stage and so on. It is the center for a variety of events.

The Yomigaeri

Yomigaeri holds that deities, men, and all that comprises nature are reborn every year. Through incessant rebirth, one's life can be maintained perpetually. The Yomigaeri, furthermore, is to gain new life particularly when united with the Musubi. Life of everything is maintained through continuous making, forming, and reviving.

The Yaoyorozu-No-Kami

In the Kami Way, there are a variety of deities referred to as the Yaoyorozu-No-Kami (eight hundred myriad deities). Here, a mountain and a river can be a deity. A sword or an accessory, even a wolf may well be a deity. The deity is placed on the extended line of nature and human beings. There is no one and only supreme being in the Kami Way. Under such a philosophy, no elder or traditional deities can claim vested rights. Since, with each new generation, new deities are discovered, it is required that the elder deities have intelligence and make strenuous efforts sufficient to meet new challenges. This state of being is, in turn, reflected in such modes of thinking that the more alternatives there are, the better ; that independence is to be promoted ; competition-restrictive practices should be abolished ; that every individual is a leading actor ; and that continual learning, training and reeducation are to be encouraged.

Many Deities as One Deity, One Deity as Many Deities

One's life and spirit were given by one's parents, whose life and spirit were, in turn, given by their parents, and on and on, so that one's life and spirit have been inherited through generations. One's ancestors were, in turn, tied with their forefathers' spirits which were strung out of the deities of life and others at the beginning of Heaven and Earth. Such a relationship is briefly comprehended in the expression 'Many Deities as One Deity, One Deity as Many Deities'. That is, it was this way of thinking that was at work in setting up community deities. This same way of thinking, furthermore, has helped people to organize a community through a community deity.

The Nigi-Mitama and the Ara-Mitama

Nigi-Mitama and Ara-Mitama represent the extreme frames of mind of a deity, respectively, the mildest and the wildest. The Nigi-Mitama shows the peaceful state of a deity's mind, while the Ara-Mitama shows its furious state. It can be said that the Nigi-Mitama is appropriate in running things in a calm environment while the Ara-Mitama manifests itself in a state of emergency. The Kami Way is superb in its sense of balance. In most cases, it can meet a situation in flexible a manner. When conditions change drastically, furthermore, it turns from Nigi-Mitama into Ara-Mitama. It is said that there is an aesthetic moment of change from Nigi-Mitama to Ara-Mitama.

The Deities and Men Co-Working

Deities and Men Co-Working originated in the tales of Kojiki. It represents the high value of working, diligence, and confidence in one's work. It also tacitly implies that the management and the workers take delight in working, and are pleased to work together. Cooperation among people, in that context, is almost synonymous with Deities and Men Co-Working.

The Communal Dining

By Communal Dining is meant that a person (or persons) dines with a deity (or deities) or that a person (or persons) dines with another person (or others). Food is, in itself, a blessing of Nature, i.e., a gift bestowed by deities. Dining is, therefore, a deed between a deity (or deities) and a person (or persons), and further a deed between a person (or persons) and another person (or others). In other words. Communal Dining is a social activity which maintains a good relationship between those participating in the activity. It is conducive in making human relations close and intimate.

The Kanjyo

Kanjyo is taking part of a deity from an existing shrine and transferring it to a new shrine. It is also the receipt of a deity's spirit from a certain shrine, and adding it to the shrine of its receiver. The shrine that thus obtains or adds a part of a deity or its spirit is called the Matsha. The Matsha is, as it were, a franchisee within a franchise system. In that way, shrines have increased in number, and now there are about 81,000 shrines nationwide.

Why have shrines increased to such an extent through Kanjyo ? It is, in the first place, due to the fact that there is no idle in the Kami Way. There is neither an idol nor a portrait of the deity. There are few commandments. In the second place, it is ascribed to the fact that there is no thought of missionary work in the Kami Way. If there appears to be divine favor shown at a certain shrine, people become devotees of that shrine. If, however, no divine favor is revealed, or people do not sense such favor, they abandon the shrine. Accordingly, shrines make all-out efforts to attract the populace. They search for and introduce a more popular and efficacious deity if the existing deity or deities are no longer appealing to the populace. In the Kami Way, there is neither only one being, nor is their Absolute Immutability. The Kanjyo, thus,

17

represents such modes of thinking and ways of viewing that eliminate a single way of thought ; things are freely introduced and improved with no restriction ; and no one should stick to some established and conventional procedures out of habit.

The Shugo

Shugo introduces doctrines or assertions from diverse sources, joining them into one whole. If one sticks to conventional doctrines or deities and lives in peace only with them, he or she begins to lose an enterprising spirit and effectiveness in his or her ways of viewing things and modes of thinking. In other words, everything stagnates and becomes impure unless new doctrines or deities are introduced to challenge and to unite themselves with the conventional ones. This is particularly so in Japan where there is a 'culture drift', being far removed from other societies by sea and by distance. Shugo solves the culture drift problem. In this way, free action and practicality, with no adherence to traditional styles, and flexibility in devising measures are characteristic of Shugo.

To sum up, the representative attributes of the Kami Way are shown concisely as in the following table.

Table 3.1   Representative attributes of the Kami Way

Musubi	Giving birth. Making and forming.
Akaki-Kokoro	Sincerity. A true heart.
Misogi	Purification-making.
Mitama-Furi	Soul-invigorating.
Hajio-Shiru-Kokoro	Shame-sensitive mind.
Kotodama	Spirit of words.
Matsuri	Trying to materialize new ideas, planning and others through an event.
Yomigaeri	Reviving. Incessant rebirth.
Yaoyorozu-No-Kami	Eight hundred myriad deities.
Many Deities as One Deity, One Deity as Many Deities	A way of thinking at work in setting up community deities.

Nigi-Mitama and Ara-Mitama	The mildest state and the wildest state of a deity's mind.
Deities and Men Co-Working	Representing the high value of working and cooperation.
Communal Dining	Representing a social activity to maintain a good human relationship.
Kanjyo	Receiving a deity's spirit from a certain shrine and adding it to the shrine of its receiver.
Shugo	Introducing doctrines or assertions from diverse sources and joining them into one whole.

3.2 Manifestations of the Kami Way attributes in history

We have so far taken up and explained the most distinctive ways of viewing things, modes of thinking and state of being of the Kami Way. Now, let us next see how the attributes of the Kami Way have been manifested in history. The following examples will serve to provide a concrete image of the attributes in the Kami Way.

Kimono, a manifestation of Shugo

Most people nowadays think that the Kimono is a thing of Japanese origin. It is, contrary to that popular belief, a representation of the things which were originally brought in from foreign countries and combined in various and distinct ways. According to K. Higuchi, a combination of pants and a jacket buttoned up in front was the commonly worn clothing among people during the Japanese neolithic cultural period. It was originally from North Asia. Later, a plain, loose one-piece garment with no sleeves was introduced from Southeast Asia, along with a rice crop agricultural technology. As a result, the clothing of northerners and southerners in Asia met for the first time in Japan. Why was the plain one-piece garment brought in together with the rice crop production technology ? It is apparently because these clothes were convenient to wear during the production of the rice crop, while a jacket and trousers were not. Over time people blended the two clothing styles. That compromise was a wadded garment, which is clothing stuffed with cotton. It took the form of a one-piece with sleeves. It was the archetype of the Kimono which appeared around the 5th century, and formed the first stage in the development of Kimono. Later, Chinese clothing of the Tang age (618-907) was introduced into Japan and came to be used as the uppermost part of women's costume. It was a jacket with narrow sleeves. Due to its popularity, the one-piece garment with sleeves people had worn was changed from outerwear to underwear. This was the second stage in the history of the Kimono. During the 15th to 16th centuries, another significant change occurred in the Kimono. The one-piece underwear with sleeves came on the stage again. That is, the one-piece underwear was remade to be longer, and its sleeves were broadened. In addition, the tie of its sash which used to be placed in front was moved to the back, and ornaments in front such as a necklace and a brooch were all absorbed into the sash. It was the third stage in the evolvement of the Kimono where today's Kimono was nearly completed. (K. Higuchi, 1988)

The Kimono is, thus, a manifestation of Shugo in that it has accumulated and combined elements of different kinds to create something new meeting the needs of people.

Imported plants and livestock, a manifestation of Kanjyo

We can see, many times in history, such a way of thinking that one is to take in whatever things new he encounters. One ought to swallow everything at first just as a whale does, and then throw out anything unnecessary later. (K. Higuhi, 1988) Almost all of the plants cultivated in Japan were originally imported from overseas. After having been imported, they have been improved in one way or another to take root domestically. Plants of native species are, indeed, very few. The native ones may be only Japanese horse-radish and Japanese radish. Even today, new kinds of plant are still imported either for decoration or for food.

In that context, the same can be said of livestock. All of the animals that the Japanese now breed such as dogs, cats, horses, cattle, pigs and chicken are of foreign species in origin. Japanese people have hardly tamed animals and made them into livestock. (K. Higuchi, 1988)

What they have done is to Kanjyo plants and livestock to enrich people's life.

Other manifestations of Kanjyo and Shugo

In the Meiji era, the Japanese emphatically introduced the Western culture and institutions. Their ways of introducing them, however, seemed to be sometimes inordinate. In 1875, there was a public notice for enlightenment which read as follows.

What a strange look, a man with the Western costume has ! He puts on a Prussian hat and has a pair of French shoes on. His jacket buttoned up in front is that of British navy's, and his trousers are from American army's formal dress.....It is just as if a Japanese were painted on his body in a mosaic way with things from different countries in the West. (H. Kato, 1968)

It would be all right for a man to wear the Western costume. But often the appearance is too odd and uneven. He should dress himself in a right and proper manner if he so wishes. That is what the above notice meant.

In spite of such an intellectual's advice, the public had their own way to combine both cultures. They worked out a blending between the Western culture and institutions and those of traditional Japan. The following are some of the cases of such a blending which appeared in the newspapers at that time.

a) A person with hair cut and let down has the Western clothing and a pair of Japanese wooden clogs on.
b) A person has the Western costume and a Japanese half-coat on.
c) A tonsured person wears the Western clothing.
d) A woman with hair cut short has a cloak on and carries an umbrella in her hand.
e) A woman with a tea-stirrer form of hair wears the Western costume.
f) A man with Western clothes wears a Japanese sword.

Among the blending above, the combination of Western clothing and Japanese wooden clogs seems to have been natural in those days. The public must have thought that it would be all right if a combination of Western clothes and Japanese wooden clogs is comfortable and convenient to wear. That's the way life is. That's the way culture is.

The Japanese have, many times in history, formed a new combination of clothes to have a healthy and convenient life, although some intellectuals have often uttered cynical remarks about them. (H. Kato, 1968)   After the Meiji Restoration when the meat-eating habits were introduced from the West, people Shugoed them in the form of sukiyaki, a dish of meat and vegetable briefly cooked. Foreign culture and institutions were introduced, i.e., Kanjyoed, and then combined with others to create new ones, i.e., Shugoed. Anpan, a bean-jam bun, and appappa, a plain one-piece dress for summer wear, are also among the examples of Kanjyo and Shugo.

Drinking sake, a manifestation of Yomigaeri

Ancient people thought that when a man is drunken, a deity goes inside of him and he becomes divinely inspired. The divine inspiration, in turn, washes away human wants and desires and returns him to the natural state. It reproduces a vigor of spirit in him. To drink sake, thus, was originally to help men to be divinely inspired to return to the nature. They drank sake to bring a spirit of nature and a spirit of deity into them. (K. Higuchi, 1988)

They drank sake for Yomigaeri.

Wrecking and reconstructing, a manifestation of Yomigaeri

In the Tokugawa era, demolishing buildings was the main way to extinguish fires. The capital city of Yedo encountered a most disastrous fire every 60 years, and had a big fire every 12 to 13 years. Whenever a great fire erupted, the city was all but destroyed due to their fire fighting methods. Citizens in Yedo, however, were not disheartened by any fire and worked hard to reconstruct the city every time it was devastated. Their reconstruction activities, in turn, stimulated the economy and thus helped their vigor of spirit recovered.

It is not the Tokugawa shogunate but the citizens of Yedo that rose like a phoenix from the ashes and rebuilt the city. (K. Higuchi, 1988)

Yomigaeri was characteristic of Yedo citizens.

A private school in the Tokugawa era, a manifestation of Yaoyorozu-No-Kami

In the Tokugawa times, there were many private schools of different kinds as well as state-administered elementary schools. What is to be noted here is that the state-administered elementary schools was originally conceived by the populace. They felt and thought it necessary out of their knowledge in life. The state administration only followed the conception.

The private school institution was established and managed by the public with no interference by the state at all. The institution was basically conceived and formed with such autonomy that both farmers and townsmen formed their own relief system. The institution of learning was, thus, autonomously run by people.

In other words, the populace, i.e., farmers, townsmen and craftsmen, were independent enough to distance themselves from the administration. What the Tokugawa shogunate did as statesmen was only to utilize people's autonomous organizing abilities, institutionalize some of their practices, and assist them in some way or other. The bureaucratic organization rested on a solid base of public autonomy. The Tokugawa shogunate, indeed, stimulated the private education institutions to develop and so exacted no tax from them. It is no exaggeration to say, therefore, that the statesmen could not have done anything without the independent and self-reliant Japanese public. (K. Higuchi, 1988)

The independence and initiative of Yaoyorozu-No-Kami (i.e., the general public) undertook a burden of education at that time.

Ancestors and the Public, manifestations of Yaoyorozu-No-Kami

Among the merchants who performed excellent business activities in the Tokugawa times were Ohmi Merchants. They started out with their business in the region of Ohmi, and expanded it throughout Japan. To a great extent, their development in business could be attributed to the regional nature of Ohmi. Ohmi was a gathering of diminutive lands which were owned by feudal lords, but geographically far distant from the main domains of those lords. Since the economy was self-sufficient at that time and transportation was underdeveloped, these distant regions were usually left loosely administered.

Thus, people in these areas had nothing to rely on but the exchange economy across borders. They launched into an inter-domain line of business and expanded it nationwide. The economic principles of no regulation and the unfettered ways of viewing and thinking were basic to them in performing business activities.

As for the business ethics, there were two concepts, 'Ancestors' and 'the Public', which were most emphasized in their merchant way. (E. Ogura, 1990) Merchants-to-be were taught, time and again, to have respect and regard to their ancestors and the general public. People thought it fundamental in the way of business to respect Yaoyorozu-No-Kami such as their ancestors and the public. It was the crux of their business ethics.

Naorai, a manifestation of Communal Dining

In the period of Tokugawa, festivals were often held at a shrine, when people made offerings such as fish, vegetables, salt, rice and sake to

23

the deities. In closing a festival, they performed a deed called 'Naorai'. The Naorai meant that deities and men turned themselves into other beings and came into harmony with each other. In the midst of a festival, the deities were far away from the place where it was being held. When the Naorai began, they descended to that place to meet men, which was referred to as the 'unification of deities and men'. The festival was formally closed after Naorai was completed.

In reality, the Naorai represents such a deed that men and deities drink and eat offerings together. (K. Higuchi, 1988) It is a form of Communal Dining or Deities and Men Co-Dining. The Naorai indicates a social deed to maintain a good relationship between deities and men, men and others, and a group of men and another.

In this context, among Japanese traditional customs, there is a practice of imparting and sharing some of one's side dish to his neighbors. In an event such as a wedding ceremony, furthermore, people drink to the health of a new couple and its participants. Those cases represent Communal Dining. The Communal Dining is still an aspect of life today.

Ko, a manifestation of Kotodama and Matsuri

The administrative laws, which were enacted from 1711 to 1716 in the Tokugawa times, stipulated that people were prohibited from holding a meeting or acting jointly without permission. However, they were allowed to do so if it was for the matters of religion since the religious authority was generally respected as in feudal societies everywhere in the world. The public, thus, had meetings among themselves on the pretext of religious matters. They used 'Ko' for such gatherings.

The Ko was an abbreviation of 'Kosha' which had originally meant an assembly to listen to a monk's lecture. Since Ko was a good means to assemble, the public came up with many kinds of Ko to get together for different purposes. In Ko, they exchanged information on the things of life and thought. Participants in Ko developed the ways and manners of companionship, and in time enhanced the thought of liberation and union. Ko was generally set out in such a way that each member of a family was to belong to a line of Ko appropriate to him or to her. Thus, information was diffused throughout the participating family members. Ko offered the public the opportunities of mutual aid and liberation from regulations as well as an exchange of information. (K. Higuchi, 1988)

Thus, the Ko is characterized by Kotodama meaning to send out, as a message, new ideas, ways of thinking, planning and others to the community of its sender, and by Matsuri that people assemble to talk about those ideas and thinking to institute an event. It is also supported by the way of Co-Dining that people share the same food. The public learned to cooperate with one another and recognized the importance of mutual aid through Ko. They were further motivated to provide unconditional services to others. In particular, they used to give charity to pilgrims. They were volunteers in today's terms.

4   The US culture

4.1 Characteristic attributes of the US culture

We have so far described how the attributes of the Kami Way have been manifested in history. Although the examples cited above are not all-inclusive, they will certainly help us to deliberate on the subject of competitiveness and culture later on.

Now, let us turn to the leading culture in the US. According to Gary P. Ferraro, there are nine noticeable attributes in the US culture. (Gary P. Ferraro, 1990)
They are the following :
1   Individualism
2   Concept of precise time
3   Deed, i.e., Profession and Diligence
4   Future-orientedness
5   Youngness, Newness
6   Taking things easy
7   Men controlling the natural world
8   Competition
9   Relative equality between men and women
To the above, the author would like to add the acceptance of immigrants as Item 10. It seems clear that people in the US have placed a primary importance on immigrants since the foundation of the state.

Individualism

The concept of an individual is firmly embedded in the social, political and economic systems in the US. It is generally agreed that the value of an individual is of prime consequence and that he or she has an ability of determining his or her courses of life. The individual is not only responsible for what he does, but he is the source of intellectual power indispensable to evaluate his deeds. People in the US spend their time and express their feelings with their family, but more extensively with such social groups as churches, schools, labor unions, companies and diverse voluntary organizations. They autonomously and actively participate in those groups.

At home, they try to teach the concept of individualism to their children and encourage them to be independent early in the childhood. Children are told to make a decision on their own, state clearly their view of value, have their own opinion, and resolve their own problems. They are encouraged not to be dependent on their teachers or parents in solving a problem but to seek it out themselves. Parents often say to their children, 'Investigate it for yourself'. That is an expression typical of Americans' desire of teaching such personal qualities as individualism and self-reliance into their children's mind.

The ideal of education in the US is not for people to serve God or the state, but to encourage them each to develop their own potential power to the fullest extent. A person's success depends on how he can develop the potential power inside him.

Concept of precise time

For Americans, time is solid and genuine in nature, and one of the essential things in life. It is treated as if it were a tangible commodity. As in the case of money, they say that they spend time, save time, earn time and waste time.

Deed, i.e., Profession and Diligence

Americans value work, activities and performance very highly. They like men's vital power, dislike laziness, and prefer a man of action to a man of thought. Protestant ethics say that a man is not merely to work for himself. His work or profession is bestowed by God. Accordingly, he is to show his real worth to God and himself through work. Work is something of integrity as well as to be respected. That way of thinking is shared among most people.

Americans have a long and unique tradition of respecting diligence. The concept of precise time described previously is to be understood in the context of diligence.

Profession, on the other hand, has a significant influence over one's identity in the American society. One's identity is very much tied to his profession. If one is discharged from his or her work, it would decisively hurt his or her pride. He might lose his self-respect to such an extent that he thinks himself an unimportant person. When a person, who has lived the same working life all through his career, has no choice but to retire, he would no doubt lose his identity. He needs to be associated with whatever activities available after retirement.

In fact, many retired Americans perform activities like collecting clothes for the poor, transforming some books into Braille ones, and engaging themselves in voluntary activities in regional hospitals, rather than being soaked in such amusement as golfing, playing bridge and others.

Future-orientedness

Americans are future-oriented. Both past and present has less meaning. While putting importance on human deed, they would think things to be future-oriented. Thus, the present is something not only improvable but to be improved for them. Future-orientedness is a source of vital power for American people.

Youngness, Newness

People in the US tend to emphasize youngness and newness. They try to keep their mind fresh. The American free-enterprise system, in that context, has stimulated people's preference for youngness and newness. Americans would discard things at hand right away if something improved or new come out on the market next year.

Youngness means to be energetic and enthusiastic about whatever things they are, characterized by wit and fully flexible ways of thinking and deed. The characteristics of youngness are essential conditions for people to become productive members of a society and contribute to its goals.

The value of future-orientedness stated above is certainly congruous with the virtues of youngness and newness.

Taking things easy (Informality)

To take things easy is characteristic of most Americans. In the early days of American history, pioneers left things of formality in their cities and towns of the East to move to frontiers in the West. There, they squarely had to face a harsh and relentless life which could not possibly be suited for those vanities and ceremonies in the East. Instead, in the West, simple and much easier practices developed in costume, a style of talking, etiquette and human relations, which have been to a considerable extent inherited to this day.

People tend to see the way of taking things easy as a necessary condition to be a person of integrity. They would be ill at ease, indeed, when they happen to encounter such ceremonies, traditions, social rules, and whatever formalities as prevailed broadly in Europe. They seem to dislike or be uncomfortable with social titles. People's detestation of social class is extensively spread in the American society.

The greater part of Americans, on the other hand, have tried hard not to obey any social position based on age, lineage and other like properties. Americans would feel irritated particularly when they see people saluting or showing whatever postures of obedience. Such behavior not only exhibits a stiff manner and something of an aristocratic snob, but implies to refuse egalitarianism.

People in the US are likely to pay respect to a company's president that mows his own lawn and, tucking up his sleeves, works together with his staff. The US is a rare country, in fact, where many students think it natural to call their university faculty by their first name.

By the way of thinking easy, people can establish a relationship with others quickly, call each other by their first name, and build friendship between them. They most often make a joke or kidding each other. Such a joke or kidding is a balancing act to make people modest, and as such plays a significant social role.

Men controlling the natural world

People in the US think that nature or the natural environment is not only controllable but to be controlled for men's benefit. If sufficient time and capital were provided, in the end, it could be controlled by men. (G. P. Ferraro, 1990) In such a way of thinking, there seems to be a solid logic.

Americans tend to logically push ahead with things and leave no room for any ambiguity of emotions. Few Americans would say, for instance, that we benevolently met the needs of the Japanese shortly after the Second World War and so Japanese people ought not to forget what we did for them.

People's solidness of logic, in turn, seems to be attributed to the multinational nature of the US. R. Shiba says,

> The strength fundamental to the multinational nature of the US is found where the feelings and emotions of people of diverse nationalities go through layers and layers of filtration in the American society. Values recognized after that filtering are so solid and genuine that they can be universally accepted. (R. Shiba, 1989)

29

If logic becomes more and more solid, it could spread and prevail everywhere on the globe.

Americans' solid logic is also reflected in the concept of freedom and its significance.

> If freedom is gone in the US, people's willingness to belong to this man-made country would vanish, and its economy would collapse. The American society would fall apart accordingly. Freedom is the source of American vital power and the light of men's hope while it is accompanied with the adverse side effects of bloody crimes. (Ibid.)

Logic of freedom is basic to American people.

Competition

Competition weighs much with people in the US. It is also affiliated with the values of individualism and performance. Most Americans, particularly men, commonly have a desire to win at whatever they do. The American system of laws, corresponding to that, is based on a principle of a competitive process. People resort to competition to keep justice. The premise of such a system is that a plaintiff and a defendant can compete each other with judicially convincing assertions, facts and precedents before a jury comes to a judgment. (G. P. Ferraro, 1990)

Here, we can see a solid logic again. Since people are of different national origins, it seems very fair to leave out their feelings and emotions, and force things forward in an exact logical way to reach a universal solution.

Relative equality between men and women

In some countries, men and women are more equal than in the US. However, it can be said that women in the US can enjoy a relatively higher social status. They have the same lawful, economic, political and social benefits as men.

Acceptance of immigrants

Since the founders first came to the land of America from England and established norms for their society, people after people of diverse origins have come and accepted those norms. New immigrants are yet coming from abroad even today. The multinationality of the US is still the fact of life.

One would hardly believe, therefore, that the US is a country with more than 200 years of history.

The youngness of America must be ascribed to its multinational nature and drastic changes caused by various reasons. (R. Shiba, 1989)

The acceptance of immigrants is, no doubt, congruent with the values of youngness and newness.

4.2 Charter of freedom

In Chapter 4, Section 1, we have taken a general view of the attributes of the US culture. Out of them, here, let us take up and make an additional remark on Competition which is very much American. Since that attribute is thought to be represented most clearly in the corresponding system of laws, we shall take up the American anti-monopoly law and the fundamental ways of thinking reflected in it.

The United States is a country of freedom. It is the anti-monopoly law, known together as the 'Anti-Trust Laws', that is the most symbolic and representative of the US. The Anti-Trust Laws is generally called the charter of freedom and an organized system of laws supporting capitalism and liberalism in the country. It is often said that the US is the homeland of an anti-monopoly law. It was not the first country, however, to establish such a law. Why is it said so, then ? It is most probably because the Anti-Trust Laws have spread themselves through the American society and been extensively and severely executed country-wide. The Anti-Trust Laws are a gathering of some Federal laws on anti-monopoly. There are such government organizations as FTC and the Department of Justice to execute them.

On the other hand, it is characteristic of the American society that a private citizen and a private enterprise play a great role in the law system. Under the Anti-Trust Laws, there are a great many suits named 'private suits' brought by private enterprises and consumers. Private suits rapidly increased in the 1960s and reached their peak in the 1970s. They have somewhat decreased since then, but there are about 1000 cases annually. That number is nearly 5 times that instituted by FTC and the Department of Justice. (T. Hasegawa, 1991)

The fact that many citizens participate in and support the law system obviously shows their awareness of laws and justice. In the US, people's concern with laws is much higher than that of other peoples.

Not too many years ago (only about 200 years ago), their ancestors founded a new country with their own system of laws. Such a knowledge is deep in their mind. If a law is rigorous and stringent in content, therefore, companies do not even regard it as a fetter to regulate their business activities. It seems that people take the Anti-Trust Laws, along with the fundamental concept behind them, as a guardian deity of freedom in the state economy.

As an example, we can cite the case of AT&T divestiture. Before the divestiture, there had been a logic of natural monopoly to vindicate the state of AT&T's monopoly. The argument for AT&T's monopoly was one of economies of scale. In other words, when the production of telecommunication equipment increases in volume, their unit cost would go down accordingly and, therefore, it was most effective for a single large company to monopolize the market. Such a protective logic had been founded on a stable market and standardized technology. But, the premises of the logic above turned out to be unfounded due to the advent of technological innovation of diverse kinds. There occurred a series of advances such as diversification of in-house telephone equipment, remarkable development of trans-mission techniques, appearance of services of non-telephone like data and image communication, and advancement in computer and electronics.

Thus, the AT&T monopoly under government regulations was no longer justified. The FCC and the court of justice decided that this natural monopoly was no longer appropriate. There had been, since then, three anti-trust suits brought by the Department of Justice against AT&T. In 1982, a reconciliation was reached between them, and the divestiture of AT&T was executed in 1984. Thus, the local telephone services in the monopolized field were divested from AT&T whereby 22 independent Bell companies were established as new entities. On the other hand, the long-distance telephone service in the non-monopolized area was succeeded by AT&T together with the field of in-house telephone equipment, advanced services and production of communication equipment and apparatus. The divestiture, therefore, put to end an unfair practices, such as profitable divisions supporting non-profitable divisions. The Bell System established by AT&T more than 100 years ago, was split into a long-distance company and several local service companies. Instead, AT&T was permitted to launch into growth areas such as computer technologies, data communication, office automation and others which are not subject to FCC's regulations. AT&T was not, therefore, altogether disadvantaged by the divestiture. Rather, it turned out to be a stout and sound company which met market changes and innovated quickly.

What was expected of that divestiture, in other words, was to build a just and free market so that telecommunication can be further improved and advanced. In enforcing the Anti-Trust Laws, like the above, it is often the case that the criteria of judgment is placed in such improvement and advancement.

The thought of anti-monopoly is also found in professional sports. It is in 1964 that the draft system was introduced into American professional baseball, having followed after the example of the professional football. In the 1950s before the draft system was adopted, it had been a golden age for the New York Yankees. During 12 years, they won the World Series 7 times. There were many people who had a strong antipathy against that state of monopoly. There were also others who thought that it was not a good state for professional baseball to develop further. When teams in rivalry compete each other in a fair way, then, people can expect the players' skill to advance and enjoy seeing a thrilling and pleasant game. That way of thought brought the draft system into practice, which corresponded to the American way of thinking that competition leads to an advancement in the society.

The anti-monopoly law is a law to secure a free and fair competition. It is thought here that competition itself is not always a good thing, but a fair competition deserves a real value.

Yet, even if people play in a fair way, abiding by rules, American people do not necessarily think it fair. In case of the professional baseball, it was regarded as unfair for a single team with extraordinary fighting power to win all the time if it did fight fairly by observing the rules. That is why the draft system was introduced to make fighting strength uniform among all the teams.

American people are likely to judge a competition fair or unfair depending on how it can be conducive to the advancement and improvement of an individual's capacity or of the society. That is a tradition since the foundation of the country, and represents part of American culture.

5 Similarities and differences between Japanese and the US cultures

In Chapter 3 and 4, we have described the leading Japanese and US cultures so that their respective attributes can be seen in a right and appropriate perspective. The readers, however, may have felt that there is a big gap between these cultures. In a way, it seems natural since the expressions used in describing each of the cultures are very different. As stated before, culture is, in essence, the modes of viewing things, the ways of thinking and the state of being of a people. It is simple and concrete in nature, and always with people in their daily life. To understand both cultures further, let us explain here the similarities and differences by citing their familiar manifestations.

Popularization of college education

The college education is broadly popularized both in Japan and the US. Why do many students go on to a college in both countries ? It seems certain that the popularization of college education may well be tied with social mobility although it is difficult to say which is the cause or its effect.

The social mobility in both countries is remarkably higher than in all the other societies including those in Europe. It is quite often the case in Japan and the US that the profession and social position in which a child will be engaged in the future may be entirely different from his or her parents. A child of a poor farmer can become a president of a large corporation. A child of a factory worker can grow to be a great scientist.

Changes of generation, therefore, could lead to the alterations of a society in some way or other. It is believed in both countries that social changes can be most facilitated by people of new generations. Such a belief is firmly embedded in Japanese and US cultures. (H. Kato, 1968)

In other words, the attributes of individualism and future-orientedness of US culture and those of Yaoyorozu-No-Kami and

Yomigaeri of Japanese culture are manifested here.

Value of newness

There is one thing which exactly agrees between the advertisements in Japan and those in the US. That is the fact that the expression 'new' is synonymous with that of 'better'. Both people think that things new have more value than things old. They are fond of something new. Newness is of value in itself. In the same way, the Japanese and Americans believe that the 'change' indicates 'progress'. A continuous cycle of construction after destruction is indicative of progress. Today's state-of-the-art products will eventually fall into commonplace tomorrow. (H. Kato, 1968)

Such a way of thinking represents an American view that youngness and newness are highly valuable. At the same time, in Japanese culture, it indicates Musubi (meaning to give birth, make and form) and Yomigaeri, a way of thinking that every thing is reborn every year.

Relationship between a State and the United States

The United States is not a nation state. There were some states in the beginning, and those states and other new ones were united afterwards into the United States. Oversimplifying the situation to make that matter clear, the United States is a federation of states. If we look for a similar country on the globe, it would not be a nation like France, Denmark and Germany, but a federation like EU. At first glance, it seems that a State's sovereignty in the US has weakened due to the expansion of Federal Government's rights. In reality, however, each State is still independent enough.

Americans have a dual attitude toward political power. On the one hand, they try to support the classical two-chamber system, limit the rights of a State's governor to a certain extent and keep the balance of power among bureaucrats. They have a tradition of disliking power whatever it is although there are much fewer reasons for them to be afraid of its misuse than for other peoples. They still have a tendency of trying to crush political power. On the other hand, when faced with a crisis, they would see political power as a necessary means and give due regard to it. (H. Kato, 1968)

There is a way of thinking shown here that a society is organized by relying on its members' self-reliance and as such it is to be maintained by all. That way of thinking is analogous to Many Deities as One Deity, One Deity as Many Deities, a representative attribute of

Japanese culture. A sense of balance is apparently reognized in that attribute. It is a superb sense of balance which is also characteristic of American culture.

Value of diligence

As was explained previously, there is a long and unique tradition of greatly respecting diligence among American people. They esteem people's vitality very much and like a man of deed while disliking a man of idleness.

Profession is of significance in that context. One's profession not only plays an indispensable role in forming his identity, but can be his identity itself. If he is relieved of his post forever, therefore, he likely loses his self-esteem and values, and eventually his identity as well. The fact that many retired Americans look for voluntary activities can be understood in the context of their putting a high value on diligence.

In the words of Japanese culture, it is expressed as a mind of Musubi. Musubi has a propensity to preference for production, where an exceedingly high value is given to the concept of work.

Taking things easy (Informality)

To take things easy is one of the essential values in the American culture. As described earlier, Americans are people who came to this land, having altogether left those ceremonies, traditions, and stiff social rules which had prevailed in Europe. In the earlier frontier age, furthermore, they intentionally discarded things of vanity and stiffness generally spread in the East, and moved on to frontiers in the West. There, they came up with their new costume, ways of talking and etiquette, and the like. Casual practices, in particular, developed in human relations which have been inherited to this day. They, accordingly, dislike social classes of any sort and tend to disregard whatever social position based on age, lineage and other personal properties. They are likely to be irritated when they encounter a formal salutation or other types of obedience posture.

Such American disposition has often been compared to the so-called Japanese salutation, their roundabout ways of expression and stiffness, which have been publicized as a major difference between both cultures. The thing is, however, that they have compared apples and oranges. Salutation, roundabout ways of expression and stiffness are characteristic of the Confucianist mentality which is only a side line of Japanese culture. As already stated, it is the Kami Way that is the leading culture in Japan.

The Kami Way mentality is not stiff nor of vanity, but free and broad-minded. Its central attribute is Akaki-Kokoro which represents 'sincerity' and 'a true heart'. The way of thinking is that everything is all right if it is done with a sincere and true heart. American people often regard taking things easy as a condition necessary for a man of integrity. Japanese people think, likewise, Akaki-Kokoro the highest among human values.

What difference, then, can we see here ?

Using first names

Americans like a president of a firm who mows lawn himself in the garden and works together with his staff in a collegial way. As was stated before, they also think it natural that college students call their professors by their first name. The US seems to be quite a rare country in that respect. Since they are likely to disregard any social position, it is not rarely the case that an executive openly tucks up his sleeves and proceeds to do his work however near the ranks he is.

There are many cases, in fact, that managers have been evaluated by their cooperation with the ranks in doing some manual labor. Through such collaboration, they can share a feeling of friendship between them, which seems to indicate a spirit of democracy. (G. P. Ferraro, 1990)

Such cooperation between managers and staff duly corresponds to the Deities and Men Co-Working, an attribute found in the Japanese culture. Deities and men work together, and they find it enjoyable to do so.

Differences in Japanese and US cultures

So far, we have chosen and seen several familiar instances of the similarities between Japanese and US cultures. It seems that there are abundant in examples.

Where, then, can we find differences between them ? Among the attributes of US culture listed earlier, there is only one attribute, in reality, which does not agree to any of the Japanese culture. It is the way of thinking that 'men control the natural world'. That way of thinking can be hardly found in the culture of Japan. The Japanese think that 'people build a relationship with nature'. They try to collaborate with nature in attaining their objectives.

In the American culture, on the other hand, it is solid logic that can be perceived behind the way of thinking that men control the natural world. People tend to persist in their logic and not temper it with any emotions. In such a multinational country as the US, the more logical things are, the more universally they would be accepted. Solid logic is manifested, for instance, in the significance of freedom shared among American people.

R. Shiba says,

> If freedom is gone in the US, people's willingness to belong to this man-made country would vanish, and its economy would collapse. The American society would fall apart eventually. Freedom is the source of American vital power and the light of men's hope while it is accompanied with the adverse side effects of bloody crimes. (R. Shiba, 1989)

The view that men control nature has produced many M&A (mergers and acquisitions) in the business world. In the extreme case, such means as LBA, i.e., Leveraged Buy-Out have been taken, which have caused the firm concerned to suffer an unrecoverable loss. Coping with such an extreme case, some regulatory rules have been formulated. In Japan, there have been some M&A, but the cases are very few as compared with those in the US. Business tie-ups between firms are, on the other hand, many in instances. There is certainly a distinct difference between the American view and the Japanese one on this point. It does not, however, seem to be too wide to bridge.

As stated in Chapter 2, culture is an object to learn. In today's favorable environment in which information of all sorts can be diffused phenomenally fast, the knowledge of culture could be carried quickly enough wherever people are willing to learn it. People's understanding of another country's culture will lead them to reconsider theirs, and in some cases possibly metamorphose it.

6 Competitiveness and culture

We have seen that there are many similarities between the Japanese and the US cultures. We have also found that there is a difference between both cultures which is, however, not impossible to bridge. Since culture is a thing to learn, its metamorphosis is not only conceivable, but could be a fact of life.

Now, we shall next turn to the relationship between competitiveness and the two cultures. That is, we address the subject of how the attributes of Japanese and American cultures are interpreted and put in perspective with the Three-Layer Structure of Competitiveness exhibited in Chapter 1.

As was already explained, the first layer of the Three-Layer Structure of Competitiveness is Logistics. Logistics consist of the following elements.

Logistics
  * Social ethos
    Promoting independence
    Pursuing fairness
    Valuing stoicism
  * Upkeep and promotion of free market (trade) system
  * Legal foundation
  * Education
  * Ethics
So, let us describe the linkage of each element above with the cultural attributes of the US and Japan.

Social ethos

In the US culture, firstly, it is Individualism that is thought basically form its social ethos. As was set forth in Chapter 4, Section 1, the concept of an individual is embedded deeply in the social, political and economic systems of the US. An individual is not only responsible for his conduct, but the source of mental power indispensable to evaluate what he does. His success depends on how he can draw out and exercise potential power in him. Everyone wishes to succeed in whatever field he or she pursues. People feel that most opportunities are equal among them. Individualism is, thus, certainly basic to American social ethos.

In the second place, there are the attributes of Youngness and Newness. Youngness is, in particular, a characteristic attribute needed for a person to be a productive member of the society in contributing to its purposes. It is tied to the third attribute, Future-orientedness, in that context, since a person with a positive stake in future is, naturally, young in mind and seeks out things new. Thus, Individualism, Youngness and Newness, and Future-orientedness are the attributes underlying the Social ethos in America.

Individualism also corresponds to Promoting independence, the most distinguished characteristic of Social ethos, along with Diligence. It fits well with Pursuing fairness. Americans appreciate diligence greatly, which is a tradition held for a long time among them, and which is congruent with Valuing stoicism as well.

How, then, are the cultural attributes of Japan affiliated with Social ethos ?

It is Musubi that is the first cultural attribute found underlying Social ethos. It implies 'giving birth', and 'making and forming'. It indicates the capacity of producing, generating and uniting. The Musubi also demonstrates the high prestige of labor. There is, secondly, Yomigaeri included here. As was described in Chapter 3, Section 1, Yomigaeri holds that deities, men, and all that comprises nature are reborn every year. Following that line of thinking, one can rise up again and again however often he or she fails. He or she could revive and produce whatever things new, i.e., doing Musubi many times over. That state of being forms the base of Social ethos.

There is Co-Working in this connection. It represents the value of working, diligence, pride and confidence in one's work. In particular, Deities and Men Co-Working implies tacitly that the management and workers strive to work for a common goal and enjoy working together. All together, Musubi, Yomigaeri, Co-Woking, and Deities and Men Co-Working are the attributes fundamental to Social ethos in Japan.

Yaoyorozu-No-Kami and Kanjyo, in that context, correspond to Promoting independence, the most significant part of Social ethos. In the Kami Way, as stated previously, there are a variety of deities referred to as the Yaoyorozu-No-Kami. New deities are, indeed, discovered with each new generation. The older deities are required to have intelligence and make strenuous efforts sufficient to meet new challenges. That state of being, in turn, leads to such modes of thinking that independence is to be promoted ; that every individual is a leading actor. Kanjyo, as described before, has been manifested in history in such a way of thinking that one is to take in greedily whatever it is when he encounters something new. It represents such modes of thinking that things are freely introduced and improved without restriction ; that the 'one and only' way of thought is eliminated. Thus, both Yaoyorozu-No-Kami and Kanjyo fit in well with Promoting independence.

Next, it is Akaki-Kokoro that is in agreement with Pursuing fairness and Valuing stoicism. As stated in Chapter 3, Section 1, Akaki-Kokoro represents sincerity and a true heart. Placing a high value on a bright and clear mind forms an ethical basis of the Kami Way.

Upkeep and promotion of free market (trade) system

As was set forth in Chapter 4, Section 1, if freedom is gone in the US, its economy would inevitably collapse. Freedom is the vital power of American people, and it is the cultural attributes of Individualism and Acceptance of Immigrants that fundamentally support it. On the other hand, in Japan, there are such attributes as Yaoyorozu-No-Kami and Kanjyo that promote freedom.

Legal foundation and Education

In the US, the value of an individual is thought the supreme. It is generally agreed that an individual has capacity sufficient to determine his courses of life. The individual is not merely responsible for his conduct, but he is the source of mental power needed to appraise its results. It is Individualism, therefore, that fundamentally backs up Legal foundation.

In Japan, on the other hand, Yaoyorozu-No-Kami is the basic attribute found conducive to Provision of legal foundation. There is no one and only supreme being at all. Things are, if it is practicable, determined in an assembly of Yaoyorozu-No-Kami.

The same can be said of Education. As described in Chapter 4, Section 1, in the US, the concept of individualism is taught children time and again, encouraging them to be self-dependent in their early days. They are told to have their own opinion, hold their view of values in an explicit way, make a decision themselves, and solve a problem of their own.

In Japan, the attributes of Yaoyorozu-No-Kami corresponds to Education. It represents such modes of thinking that independence is to be promoted; that competition-restrictive practices should be abolished; that every individual is a leading actor ; that continual learning, training and reeducation are to be encouraged.

Ethics

Fundamental to Ethics in the US, Diligence exists as well as Individualism. People's work is worth respecting and something of integrity. It is unanimously agreed. In Japan, on the other hand, such cultural attributes are in agreement with Ethics as Misogi, Yomigaeri and Value of Cleanness, and Hajio-Shiru-Kokoro.

Misogi is a spiritual exercise in the Kami Way, and represents the ethical view that purity is of the highest value. It is to wash away dirt from one's mind in a clean water, and to revive and recover his value of cleanliness.

Hajio-Shiru-Kokoro literally means 'the shame-sensitive mind'. Its state of being is briefly comprehended in such expressions as 'Come to yourself' ; 'The Heaven knows, the Earth knows, One knows' ; 'The Heaven sees everything'.

To sum up, we can show in a table form the relationship between the elements of Logistics, the first layer of the Three-Layer Structure of Competitiveness, and the corresponding attributes of both Japanese and US cultures as follows.

Table 6.1   Competitiveness elements and US cultural attributes

I Logistics	Attributes of American culture
· Social ethos	Individualism, Youngness and Newness, Future- orientedness
Promoting independence	Individualism
Pursuing fairness	Individualism, Diligence
Valuing stoicism	Diligence
· Upkeep and promotion of free market (trade) system	Individualism, Acceptance of Immigrants
· Legal foundation	Individualism
· Education	Individualism
· Ethics	Individualism, Diligence

Table 6.2   Competitiveness elements and Japanese cultural attributes

I   Logistics   Attributes of Japanese culture

   • Social ethos   Musubi, Yomigaeri and Musubi
                                        Co-Working, Deities and Men
                                        Co-Working
    Promoting independence   Yaoyorozu-No-Kami, Kanjyo
    Pursuing fairness   Akaki-Kokoro
    Valuing stoicism   Akaki-Kokoro
   • Upkeep and promotion of   Yaoyorozu-No-Kami,
    free market (trade) system   Kanjyo
   • Legal foundation   Yaoyorozu-No-Kami
   • Education   Yaoyorozu-No-Kami
   • Ethics   Misogi, Yomigaeri and
                                          Value of Cleanliness,
                                        Hajio-Shiru-Kokoro

Now, let us next take up the second and the third layers of the Three-Layer Structure of Competitiveness to see their relationship with the cultural attributes of both countries.

The second layer is Economic Base which consists of the following elements.

II   Economic Base
     • Infrastructure
     • Build-up of investment
     • Environmental improvement and conservation
     • Diffusion of new ideas, planning and others

The third layer is Management System which is composed of the following.

III Management System
 A. Effectiveness
  · Freely and openly introducing and developing
    new technologies and systems
  · Abolishing competition-restrictive practices
  · Activating communication
  · Commercializing technology
  · Encouraging competitive spirit
  · Others
 B. Tense balance between effectiveness and ethics
  · Organizing techniques
  · Organization where workers are little conscious
    of an organizational stratum
  · Encouraging initiative
  · Using flexible methods that can meet any situation
  · Decision-making processes with a variety of
    alternatives
  · Opportunity for continual education and
    training
  · Others
 C. Ethics
  · View of purity
  · Fair practices
  · Diligence
  · Workers as leading actors
  · Pride and self-confidence in work
  · Ethics of management-worker relations
  · Others

Diffusion of new ideas, planning and others

In the US, they generally think that new ideas, planning and others can be effectively diffused by competition. That is, new ideas, invention, contrivances and the like are disseminated through a logical and competitive mechanism.

In the Japanese culture, on the other hand, it is thought Kotodama and Matsuri which duly promote that diffusion. As described in Chapter 3, Section 1, Kotodama is literally 'the spirit of words'. It is sent out as a message to the community of its sender, while it is transmitted from one community to another to convey some important information. The Kotodama helps propagate new ideas, ways of thinking, planning and the like throughout a society.

44

Matsuri, on the other hand, originates in the event described in the Kojiki that the deities assembled, worked out a painstaking plan and finally brought it to fruition. It is, therefore, to try to materialize new ideas, planning and others through an event.

Needless to say, in this context, the competition plays a significant role in diffusing things in the market economy. No one argues against the logical and competitive mechanism needed in that dissemination. The thing is that we only narrow down the subject here to cultural attributes.

Effectiveness

As duly affiliated with Effectiveness, in the first place, there is the Concept of Precise Time in the US. Time is, as stated previously, treated exactly the same way as money. Time can be used, wasted, spent, saved and given in a man's life. It is mostly equal among people like opportunities, and precious in essence.

There are, secondly, Youngness and Newness, and Future-orientedness. American people will most likely throw things of theirs away if they come to know the new versions or improved ones appearing next year. They usually see the present not only improvable, but to be improved. That way of thinking, certainly, has much to do with Youngness and Newness, and Future-orientedness.

Competition is, next, stressed all the time in attaining a better life. Everyone has a desire to succeed in whatever he or she does. Effectiveness can be, thus, enhanced through competition.

In the Japanese culture, on the other hand, Yaoyorozu-No-Kami, Kanjyo and Shugo are the attributes that pertinently support Effectiveness. Yaoyorozu-No-Kami represents such ways of thinking that the more alternatives there are, the better ; that competition-restrictive practices should be abolished. Kanjyo has, on the other hand, such a way of thinking that one should introduce things new whatever they are, while Shugo is to try to assemble the merits of things old and those of things new with no restriction whatsoever.

In addition to those three attributes above, there are also Matsuri, as activating communication, and Mitama-Furi, in encouraging competitive spirit, underlying Effectiveness. As was set forth in Chapter 3, Section 1, Mitama-Furi is typically manifested in such an incantatory act that people carry a portable shrine on their shoulders in a shrine festival.

45

In the US, the attribute of Taking Things Easy (Informality) is thought to fit in well with the category of Tense balance between effectiveness and ethics. As was stated in Chapter 4, Section 1, Taking Things Easy is one of the crucial ingredients of the American value system. Most people have a tendency to pay respect to a president of a company that does lawn mowing himself at home, and feels free and easy to work together with his staff in office. Taking Things Easy, therefore, helps to create an organization where workers are little conscious of an organizational stratum.

American people often talk with each other in a joking or a kidding way. Joking or kidding is a balancing act in their social life, rendering people to notice the importance of humility. The attribute of Taking Things Easy represents a superb sense of balance in that respect.

Along with that attribute, furthermore, there are Competition and Individualism that have a due role in attaining a balance between effectiveness and ethics.

In the Japanese culture, it is Nigi-Mitama and Ara-Mitama, in the first place, that backs up the Tense balance between effectiveness and ethics. As was described in Chapter 3, Section 1, Nigi-Mitama and Ara-Mitama represents a deity's extreme frames of mind (the mildest and the wildest). Nigi-Mitama shows the peaceful state of a deity's mind while Ara-Mitama shows its furious state. The Kami Way is superb in its sense of balance. In most cases, it can meet a situation in flexible a manner. When conditions change drastically, however, it turns from Nigi-Mitama into Ara-Mitama. Thus, the balance can be duly kept in order.

There is, next, Yaoyorozu-No-Kami. It helps, together with Kanjyo, to form an organization where workers are barely conscious of an organizational stratum, facilitate a decision-making process with a variety of alternatives, and promote continued education, training and reeducation.

There is also Many Deities as One Deity, One Deity as Many Deities which is an attribute especially conducive to organizing techniques. As was explained in Chapter 3, Section 1, it is that attribute which was at work in setting up community deities. The main line of its logic is as follows. One's life and spirit were provided by his parents, whose life and spirit were, in turn, given by their parents, and on and on, so that one's life and spirit were inherited through generations of ancestors. One's ancestors were, in turn, tied in with their forefathers' spirits which were strung out of the deities of life and others at the beginning of Heaven and Earth. Such a relationship is generally understood in the expression 'Many Deities as One Deity, One Deity as Many Deities'. That attribute of balance is instrumental in forming a community, and also in striking a balance between effectiveness and ethics.

To be added here, finally, there is Mitama-Furi which universally encourages initiative.

Ethics

Individualism, Diligence and Competition are fundamental to Ethics among American people. As was set out in Chapter 4, Section 1, the concept of an individual is deeply rooted in the social, political and economic systems in the US. The individual is responsible for whatever he does, while he is thought to have sufficient capacity to judge the results of his conduct. No doubt, Individualism is the core of thought on ethics.

American people also like a man of vitality and dislike a man of idleness. According to Protestant ethics, a man works not just for himself. His work or profession is bestowed by God. What he does through work, therefore, is to show the true worth of his to God as well as to himself. The American have a way of thinking that work is not only worth respecting, but something of integrity. Most retired Americans would be engaged in such activities as collecting clothes for the poor, turning some books into Braille for the blind, performing volunteer activities in regional hospitals and the like. Diligence is, thus, the essential part of their life.

Competition, next, is integral to Ethics. The American judicial system is based on the process of competition. They basically rely upon competition to keep up the legitimacy of the judgment. The premise underlying that law system is that a plaintiff and a defendant can compete with each other by putting forth the best possible assertions, the most valuable facts and precedents before a jury of peers comes to a legitimate judgment. The judgment thus made is generally thought impartial and fair.

Finally, an ethically good relationship between managers and workers is considerably facilitated by the attribute of Taking Things Easy.

Now, in the Japanese culture, Ethics is descriptively expressed in the attributes of Misogi and Hajio-Shiru-Kokoro. As was put forth in Chapter 3, Section 1, Misogi is to wash away evils attached to a man with a clean water, while Hajio-Shiru-Kokoro represents the shame-sensitive mind, shown in such expressions as 'Come to yourself' ; 'The

Heaven knows, the Earth knows, One knows' ; 'The Heaven sees everything'. After performing Misogi, furthermore, one can recover Value of Cleanliness, doing Yomigaeri eventually.

There are, secondly, Co-Working, and Deities and Men Co-Working. Those attributes could help promote one's diligence, enhance one's pride and self-confidence in his or her work, and form a good relationship between the management and workers.

Finally, it is Yaoyorozu-No-Kami that sees workers as leading actors. It pertinently corresponds to Individualism among the American cultural attributes.

Taken together, the attributes of American and Japanese cultures are aligned correspondingly to the elements of the second and the third layers of Three-Layer-Structure of Competitiveness in a table form as follows.

Table 6.3   Competitiveness elements and US cultural attributes

Three-Layer Structure of Competitiveness	Attributes of American culture
II. Economic Base	
• Infrastructure	
• Build-up of investment	
• Environment improvement and conservation	
• Diffusion of new ideas, planning and others	Competition
III. Management System	
A. Effectiveness	Concept of Precise Time
• Freely and openly introducing and developing new technologies and systems	Youngness and Newness, Future-orientedness
• Abolishing competition-restrictive practices	Competition
• Activating communication	Competition
• Commercializing technology	Competition
• Encouraging competitive spirit	Competition
• Others	

48

B. Tense balance between
effectiveness and ethics   Taking Things
                                            Easy
  • Organizing techniques   Taking Things
                                            Easy
  • Organization where workers are   Taking Things
    little conscious of an organizational   Easy
    stratum
  • Encouraging initiative   Competition
  • Using flexible methods that can   Taking Things
    meet any situation   Easy
  • Decision-making processes with   Competition
    a variety of alternatives
  • Opportunity for continual   Individualism
    education and training
  • Others
C. Ethics   Individualism
                                            Diligence
  • View of purity   Competition
  • Fair practices   Individualism
                                            Competition
  • Diligence   Diligence
  • Workers as leading actors   Individualism
  • Pride and self-confidence   Diligence
    in work
  • Ethics of management-   Taking Things
    worker relations   Easy
  • Others

Table 6.4   Competitiveness elements and Japanese cultural attributes

Three-Layer Structure of Competitiveness	Attributes of Japanese culture
II. Economic Base	
• Infrastructure	
• Build-up of investment	
• Environmental improvement and conservation	The taboo of Kegare, Value of Cleanliness
• Diffusion of new ideas, planning and others	Kotodama, Matsuri
III. Management System	
A. Effectiveness	Yaoyorozu-No-Kami, Kanjyo, Shugo
• Freely and openly introducing and developing new technologies and systems	Kanjyo, Shugo
• Abolishing competition-restrictive practices	Yaoyorozu-No-Kami
• Activating communication	Matsuri
• Commercializing technology	Kanjyo, Shugo
• Encouraging competitive spirit	Mitama-Furi, Shugo
• Others	
B. Tense balance between effectiveness and ethics	Nigi-Mitama, Ara-Mitama
• Organizing techniques	Many Deities as One Deity, One Deity as Many Deities
• Organization where workers are little conscious of an organizational stratum	Kanjyo, Yaoyorozu-No-Kami
• Encouraging initiative	Mitama-Furi, Kanjyo
• Using flexible methods that can meet any situation	Nigi-Mitama, Ara-Mitama

· Decision-making process with a variety of alternatives	Yaoyorozu-No-Kami
· Opportunity for continual education and training	Yaoyorozu-No-Kami
· Others	
C. Ethics	Misogi, Hajio-Shiru-Kokoro
· View of purity	Yomigaeri, Value of Cleanliness
· Fair practices	Yomigaeri, Value of Cleanliness
· Diligence	Co-Working
· Working as leading actors	Yaoyorozu-No-Kami
· Pride and self-confidence in work	Co-Working Deities and Men Co-Working
· Ethics of management-worker relations	Co-Working, Deities and Men Co-Working
· Others	

7 What is enterprise competitiveness ?

In Chapter 1, we have accounted for the Three-Layer Structure of Competitiveness, a macro framework and criteria in reviewing the competitiveness of a state. It consists of three layers. The first layer is Logistics, the second layer is Economic Base and the third is Management System. All the layers have, respectively, competitiveness elements of their own which altogether form the state of competitiveness. In Chapter 2 through 5, we turned to culture. We have described in some details the characteristics of Japanese culture and those of American culture, and further explored the similarities and differences between the cultures of the two countries. There are many similarities and only one difference between them.

Based upon the description and findings in Chapter 1 through 5, we have then reviewed the cultural attributes of both countries in the context of competitiveness, and have come up with a relationship between those attributes and the elements of competitiveness. That relationship has been finally summed up in a table form as the attributes of Japanese and American cultures vis-a-vis the elements of Three-Layer Structure of Competitiveness. We have thus put competitiveness and the cultures of both countries in perspective.

Now, we shall next turn to the main theme of the book, enterprise competitiveness and corporate culture. Enterprise competitiveness is the competitiveness of a firm. It is formed and supported by its constituents. The constituents have, in turn, cultural attributes characteristic of their country reflected in their modes of viewing things, ways of thinking and state of being. Corporate culture is, on the other hand, the personality of a firm. Yet, it is the cultural factors ascribed to people of a firm that form its personality. The combination and strength degree of each of these attributes differ from one company to another. That difference, in reality, represents the corporate culture of a company, i.e., its personality.

To explain the above fully and orderly, we shall first describe the micro framework of enterprise competitiveness here in Chapter 7 and then address corporate culture in Chapter 8.

7.1 Three-layer structure of enterprise competitiveness

Competitiveness is the power to maintain stable and long-term predominance in a just and free market economy. Accordingly, the foundation for competitiveness is an enterprise ethos originating in the establishment of an enterprise, where every member is willing to grapple with any situation without fear of failure, and where people in the workplace freely exchange their views and opinions. Following the enterprise ethos are elements derived from and upheld by that ethos in tandem, as a way to enhance initiative, normalization, preparation of investment conditions, enterprise ethics and education. As a whole, they may well be considered 'Enterprise Logistics'.

Enterprise Logistics are required as circumstantial conditions, so to speak, but are not part of the competitiveness base per se. An enterprise has to prepare that base on its own. One such base is generally termed the 'infrastructure', which is composed of two lines. One line consists of physical assets such as facilities, machinery, networks and the like. The other line consists of human resources such as executives, scientists, engineers, skilled workers and the like. Next, what is indispensable for an enterprise to continually grow and develop is environmental improvement and conservation. This includes conservation of the natural environment, cooperation with and participation in a community and its activities, concern with cultural activities, etc. and it also includes the environment of the workplace, employee welfare and so on. The final element of that base is the diffusion of new ideas, planning and others. New ideas, reform, improvement, and intelligence about new products come into practical use only when they can be diffused, without restriction, both within and without an enterprise organization. The mechanism and the speed of that diffusion are, specifically, of consequence for an enterprise's effective performance. Taken together, let us name those elements of competitiveness listed above the 'Enterprise Economic Base'.

Once Enterprise Logistics and the Enterprise Economic Base are established, competitiveness can enter the arena for actors. The first focus on enterprise activities is effectiveness. There are many subjects to be solved in attaining effectiveness, like how to commercialize technology, how to improve cost, quality and delivery terms simultaneously, how to make communication active within and without the enterprise, how to develop, introduce and make use of technology in gaining strategic predominance, how to enhance a spirit of competitiveness and so on. Next, there is ethics which is, in a sense, in opposition to effectiveness. In this category are included such views that every member of a company is a leading actor and that diligence is highly valued in their work ; fair employment ; and just and fair chances of promotion provided to any personnel.

In this context, there are quite a few instances in the real world where a viable alternative can only be found in the area between effectiveness and ethics. For example, there are cases where an enterprise attempts to maintain close relations with customers to understand their real needs ; or that it maintains exceedingly close contact with suppliers in order to attain much higher effectiveness. In both cases, such a close contact and relationship might, unexpectedly and mistakenly, deviate from the fairness of business dealings and deteriorate into compromise and protective procedures. Therefore, the first priority is, at all times, to be placed on the mechanism of the free market system in order for those policies not to harm effectiveness. Also, elements like the development of individual abilities, a re-education system and long-term employment guarantees do not contribute directly to effectiveness from a short-term perspective. They do exert a positive influence, from a long-term perspective, on such qualitative factors as workers' pride and confidence, which, in turn, lead to enhancement of effectiveness. The policies or elements above could be, in other words, established only on the tense balance between effectiveness and ethics. The balance is tense in that those policies or elements must be severed from compromise, protectionism, unfair relations, favoritism, etc. Taken together, these elements blend into themselves to produce the 'Management System'.

To sum up, enterprise competitiveness is composed of three layers. We will term it the Three-Layer Structure of Enterprise Competitiveness, and show it in the following figure.

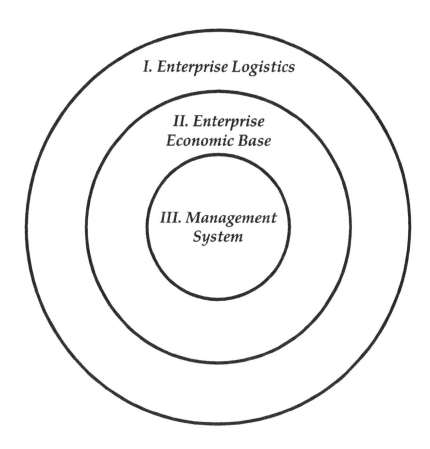

**Figure 7.1 Three-Layer Structure of Enterprise
Competitiveness**

The Structure of Enterprise Competitiveness is composed of three layers. The first layer includes Enterprise Logistics. It is the outermost layer, surrounding the second and third layers. The second layer is the Enterprise Economic Base. This is the layer that supports the arena for actors, i.e., the Management System. The third layer is, then, the Management System. It rests at the core of the Three-Layer Structure and at the center of enterprise competitiveness.

The elements of enterprise competitiveness are, in turn, shown as in the following table.

Table 7.1   Elements of enterprise competitiveness

I   Enterprise Logistics
- Enterprise ethos
  Ethos originated in the early days of an enterprise maintained.
  Every member is willing to grapple with any situation without hesitation and without worrying about failure.
  People in the workplace freely exchange their views and opinions.
- Enhancement of initiative
  There is teamwork among personnel.
  Personnel have pride and confidence in upholding their enterprise's competitiveness.
  Personnel have a sense of representing their enterprise.
  Diligence and positive activities of personnel.
  Pride and confidence in employee's own work.
  Self-reforming abilities.
- Provision of norms
  Law (company regulations, etc.).
  Spirit of the Anti-Monopoly Act.
  Ethics of relations between management and workers.
  Abolishment of practices restricting competition.
- Preparation of investment conditions
  Allows a sufficiently long time frame for management.
  Promotion of R&D and production-process R&D.
  Constraints on speculative purchases of enterprises.
- Enterprise ethics
- Education

II   Enterprise Economic Base
  • Infrastructure
  Physical assets   Facilities, machinery, network.
  Human resources   Executives, scientists,
                                 engineers, skilled workers.
  Employment of human resources and procurement of physical
  assets to build and stabilize Infrastructure.
  High investment in the training of personnel.
  (build-up of human resources)
  Education on practical business.
  • Environmental improvement and conservation
  Conservation of natural environment.
  Cooperation with and participation in a community and its
  activities.
  Concern with cultural activities. (serving a community, etc.)
  Improvement of physical environment of the workplace.
  Attention and care to human relations in the workplace.
  • Diffusion of new ideas, planning and others
  To create smooth communication.
  Managers make it a practice to talk to workers about policies
  and the state of affairs of their enterprise.
  New ideas, reform, improvement, and intelligence on new
  products are diffused smoothly both within and without the
  organization.

III Management System
  A. Effectiveness
    • Maintain a free market principle throughout an enterprise.
    • Encouraging competitive spirit.
    • Improve cost, quality and delivery terms simultaneously.
    • Development, introduction and use of technology in gaining
      strategic predominance.
    • Commercializing technology.
    • Activating communication throughout.
  B. Tense balance between effectiveness and ethics
    • Having close relationship with customers.
    • Having intimate contact with suppliers.
    • Organizing techniques.
    • Organization whose workers are barely conscious of
      organizational stratum.
    • Recognition of quality as the end result of overall production.

- The more alternatives there are in a decision-making process, the better.
- Demand and expect personnel to do their best.
- Have the capacity to flexibly cope with problems.
- Education and training, the development of personnel's abilities, continual learning.
- Long-term employment guarantee.

C. Ethics
- Every member is a leading actor.
- A view on work in which diligence is highly esteemed.
- Improvement of ethics in quality.
- Fair employment.
- Appropriate transfer of personnel from one post to another.
- Secure just and fair promotion of personnel.

Now, then, to elaborate further on the Three-Layer Structure of Enterprise Competitiveness, we will here refer to *The Competitive Advantage of Nations* by Michael E. Porter. If a nation comes to be driven by wealth-consciousness, not by innovation, he argues,

> Firms begin to lose competitive advantage in international industries for a variety of reasons...Employees lose motivation...Management-labor relations harden... Under increasing pressure, labor-management relations deteriorate further and undermine innovation even more...there are rising calls for government support and intervention that blunt dynamism still further. (Ibid. P 556-558)

As is well seen, what is pointed out here corresponds, in a converse way, to Enterprise ethos, Enhancement of initiative and Provision of norms of Logistics, the Three-Layer Structure of Enterprise Competitiveness. He further remarks,

> The prestige of working in industry may fall...chronic under- investment in industry is an ironic manifestation of a wealth driven economy...Investment in financial assets supplants investment in real assets. A symptom that may accompany a move to the wealth-driven stage is widespread mergers and acquisitions...Mergers may also reflect an increasing desire to reduce rivalry and increase stability. (Ibid. P 557)

Here, his remark relates to Ethics (A view on work in which diligence is highly esteemed) of Management System, Infrastructure (Physical assets and Human resources) of Enterprise Economic Base and Preparation of investment conditions (Constraints on speculative purchase of enterprises) of Enterprise Logistics. He thus insists,

> A company should actively seek out pressure and challenge, not try to avoid them....
> Some of the ways of doing so are the following :
> 1 Sell to the most sophisticated and demanding buyers and channels....
> 2 Seek out the buyers with the most difficult needs....
> 3 Establish norms of exceeding the toughest regulatory hurdles or product standards...
> 4 Source from the most advanced and international home-based suppliers....
> 5 Treat employees as permanent....
> 6 Establish outstanding competitors as motivators....
>
> (Ibid. PP 585-586)

Items 1 and 2 above have bearing on Tense balance between effectiveness and ethics (Having close relationship with customers) of Management System. Item 3 is related to Provision of norms of Enterprise Logistics while Item 4 has relevance to Effectiveness (Maintain a free market principle throughout an organization) of Management System. Item 5 is, on the other hand, concerned with Tense balance between effectiveness and ethics (Long-term employment guarantee), and Item 6 relates to Effectiveness (Encouraging competitive spirit).   Overall, he argues,

> What is in many ways most necessary in the United States is a philosophical shift... A return to some neglected historical values, of individual initiative, education, competition, long-term investment, tough regulation, and free trade, is long overdue. (Ibid. P 733)

It seems that his overall view, after having studied ten nations from competitiveness perspective, well fits the concept of the Three-Layer Structure of Enterprise Competitiveness. It may well be, therefore, that the Micro Model is to be applied extensively.

Next, let us touch a bit here on one of the typical cases where companies fail due to the lack of some of the decisive elements of competitiveness. Success stories are abundant and well known. There is no secret to success in a way. There is, however, real secret and much to learn in failure. A short case study explanation would serve as a good foundation to further understanding. The company we take up is Japan Airlines Co., Ltd.

Before it was transformed into a purely private enterprise in December, 1987, Japan Airlines Co., Ltd. had been a semi-governmental corporation with management intervention from the political circle and the government agency concerned. Some managers took the restructuring of their corporation seriously, indeed, and looked forward to its 'privatization'. The privatization meant to them breaking a path to independence with no protection whatsoever from the government. One of the managers said,

> As it is, there are no sense of management risk, no ground nor recognition in common for management. On such managerial matters as appointment of top management, corporate planning and even purchasing of aircraft, we have to ask for instructions from the government agency. With that sort of practice, who can take responsibility for management ? Who can expect the personnel to accumulate management skills ? (H. Okumura, K. Sasako, M. Sataka and Others, 1994)

Another middle manager said,

> If the company has become a private enterprise, it will have some difficulty with management. It will not be permitted to issue government-guaranteed debentures, for instance. However, we can expect that there will occur a thorough transformation of attitudes and thinking among the personnel, creating a lively workplace. In short, we would rise up and choose our boss among ourselves. (Ibid.)

It is apparent that there is willingness among some managers to free themselves from dependence on the political circle and the government agency concerned, and attain independence and autonomy. They would like to turn the conventional weak constitutional corporate structure into a solid, purely private organization.

As is implied above, Japan Airlines Co., Ltd., before its privatization, lacked several decisive elements of competitiveness. In the first place, it lacked Enterprise ethos (Every member is willing to deal with any situation), Enhancement of initiative and Provision of norms (Spirit of the Anti-Monopoly Act and abolishment of practices restricting competition) of Enterprise Logistics. Secondly, it is devoid of Ethics (Every member is a leading actor) of Management System. As will be shown later, in this context, the elements above correspond to such Kami Way's ingredients as Yaoyorozu-No-Kami, Akaki-Kokoro, Many Deities as One deity, One Deity as Many Deities, and Co-Working. It can well be said, therefore, that Japan Airlines Co., Ltd., lacked some of the decisive elements of the Kami Way. Thus, the transformation from its weak constitutional structure seems to be difficult to attain or to take a long time. Even after its privatization in 1987 (although it is not virtually a pure private enterprise since a majority of its shares are still in the government's hands), Japan Airlines Co., Ltd. showed a deficit in its yearly statement of accounts for three consecutive years (1990 to 1993).

8　What is corporate culture ?

Now, then, let us address the other part of the main theme of the book, corporate culture. We shall first explain its theoretical background and then take up several firms with characteristic corporate cultures.

8.1 Theories on corporate culture

Quite recently, at the end of the 1970s, corporate culture became an area of study in the field of business administration. In that period, there were corporate culture assessment attempts at leading universities (Harvard, Stanford and MIT) and at the consulting firms (Mckinsey and MAC). What is common among their assessments are the following. (J. P. Kotter and J. L. Heskett, 1992)

1　Corporate culture can have a significant impact on a firm's long-term economic performance.
2　Corporate culture will probably be an even more important factor in determining the success or failure of firms in the next decade.
3　Corporate cultures that inhibit strong long-term financial performance are not rare ; they develop easily, even in firms that are full of reasonable and intelligent people.

In this connection, books on corporate culture were successively published in 1981 and 1982 as follows.

Theory Z	by W. Ouchi 1981
The Art of Japanese Management	by R. T. Pascale and A. G. Athos 1981
Corporate Cultures	by T. E. Deal and A. A. Kennedy 1982
In Search of Excellence	by T. Peters and R. H. Waterman 1982

The books above succeeded in publication, which induced further research on corporate culture. The research following, in turn, came up with several theories on the relationship between corporate culture and performance.

According to J. P. Kotter and J. L. Heskett, these theories can be broadly classified into the following three.

Theory   I   Strong cultures
Theory   II   Strategically appropriate cultures
Theory   III   Adaptive cultures

Now, let us explain each of them, respectively.

Theory I

Firms with strong cultures seem to outsiders to have a certain style in doing business. For instance, one can see such a style in the ways and manners that Procter & Gamble and Johnson & Johnson performed business in the period from 1976 to 1986. Such firms put up values to be shared among them in their creed or mission statement, and encourage all the managers to abide by the values. The managers of those firms, therefore, have a tendency of marching in a very well-coordinated way in the same direction. Their performance can not be enhanced, however, unless their common deeds and ways of doing business are appropriate to the needs of the market for products and services, or fit in with the needs of financial and labor markets. Companies with strong cultures are also disposed to be arrogant, inward-looking, political and bureaucratic.

J. P. Kotter and J. L. Heskett, in that context, tried to decide if there is correlation between culture strength and long-term economic performance. Their approach was, first, to get a large and diverse sample of companies, i.e., picking 207 firms from 22 different US industries. The measures of performance used here were average yearly increase in net income, average yearly return on investment and average yearly increase in stock price. Second, using a questionnaire survey, they constructed 'culture strength' indices for all of those firms. After having gathered such data and analyzing it, they came up to the following statement.

> Within the limits of this methodology, we conclude from this study that there is a positive relationship between strength of corporate culture and long-term economic performance, but it is a modest relationship. 'Strong cultures create excellent performance' appears to be just plain wrong. (Ibid, P 21)

There were good performers, in this connection, among firms with weak cultures. It seemed that they may have performed well due to their monopolistic market position or relative autonomy.

Now, for the readers' reference, we shall cite an example of the assertion of Theory I. T. J. Peters and R. H. Waterman, Jr. argues as follows (*In Search of Excellence*, 1982):

> As we worked on research of our excellent companies, we were struck by the dominant use of story, slogan, and legend as people tried to explain the characteristics of their own great institutions. All the companies we interviewed, from Boeing to McDonald's, were quite simply rich tapestries of anecdote, myth, and fairy tale. And we do mean fairy tale. The vast majority of people who tell stories today about T. J. Watson of IBM have never met the man or had direct experience of the original more mundane reality. Two HP engineers in their mid-twenties recently regaled us with an hour's worth of 'Bill and Dave' (Hewlett and Packard) stories. We were subsequently astonished to find that neither had seen, let alone talked to, the founders. These days, people like Watson and A. P. Giannini at Bank of America take on roles of mythic proportions that the real persons would have been hard-pressed to fill. Nevertheless, in an organizational sense, these stories, myths, and legends appear to be very important, because they convey the organization's shared values, or culture. Without exception, the dominance and coherence of culture proved to be an essential quality of the excellent companies. Moreover, the stronger the culture and the more it was directed toward the marketplace, the less need was there for policy manuals, organization charts, or detailed procedures and rules. In these companies, people at all levels know what they are supposed to do in most situations because the handful of guiding values is crystal clear. One of our colleagues is working with a big company recently thrown together out of a series of mergers. He says : 'You know, the problem is every decision is being made for the first time. The top people are inundated with trivia because there are no cultural norms'. By contrast, the shared values in the excellent companies are clear, in large measure, because the mythology is rich. Everyone at Hewlett-Packard knows that he or she is supposed to be innovative. Everyone at Procter & Gamble knows that product quality is the sine qua non...Poorer-performing companies often have strong cultures, too, but dysfunctional ones. They are usually focused on internal politics rather than on the customer, or they focus on 'the numbers' rather than on the product and the people who make and sell it. The top companies, on the other hand, always seem to recognize what the companies that set only financial targets don't know or don't deem important. The excellent companies seem to understand that every man seeks meaning. (Ibid. PP 75-76)

They say that excellent companies have coherent and strong corporate culture. There are some cases, on the other hand, that poor-performing companies have strong culture as well which is, they say, dysfunctional. Little explanation is given, however, on the relationship between strong culture and organizational functionality. Next, they proceed to the argument on changing an organization structure.

> Perhaps transcendence is too grand a term for the business world, but the love of product at Cat, Bechtel, and J&J comes very close to meriting it. Whatever the case, we find it compelling that so many thinkers from so many fields agree on the dominating need of human beings to find meaning and transcend mundane things... Some of the riskiest work we do is concerned with altering organization structures. Emotions run wild and almost everyone feels threatened. Why should that be ? The answer is that if companies do not have strong notions of themselves, as reflected in their values, stories, myths, and legends, people's only security comes from where they live on the organization chart. Threaten that, and in the absence of some grander corporate purpose, you have threatened the closest thing they have to meaning in their business lives. So strong is the need for meaning, in fact, that most people will yield a fair degree of latitude or freedom to institutions that give it to them. The excellent companies are marked by very strong cultures, so strong that you either buy into their norms or get out. There's no halfway house for most people in the excellent companies. One very able consumer marketing executive told us, 'You know, I deeply admire Procter & Gamble. They are the best in the business. But I don't think I could ever work there.' She was making the same point that Adam Myerson at The Wall Street Journal had in mind when he urged us to write an editorial around the theme : 'Why we wouldn't want to work for one of our excellent companies.' The cultures that make meanings for so many repel others. (Ibid. PP 76-77)

The culture of an excellent company is so strong that the constituents of the company have to sacrifice a great degree of their latitude or freedom to it. There are only two alternatives for them. One is that they blindly trust and follow the company's way of business, and the other is that they decide to leave, not to join it. Thus, excellent companies sound like an organization of secular religious cult.

> Some who have commented on our research wonder if there is not a trap or two in the very strength of the structures and cultures of the well-run companies. There probably is. First, the conventions are so strong that

the companies might be blindsided by dramatic environmental change. This is a fair point. But we would argue that in general the excellent company values almost always stress being close to the customer or are otherwise externally focused. Intense customer focus leads the prototypical excellent company to be unusually sensitive to the environment and thus more able to adapt than its competitors. (Ibid. PP 77-78)

They use the word 'strong' as the synonymous with the word 'excellent'. Yes, excellent firms have such attributes as they refer to. But, it is not clear at all how those attributes are related to strong culture. In addition, how could such an organization like a religious cult with strong creed be adaptive to the environment all the time ? They provided no answer to that question. They go on to the possible abuse of strong culture.

For us, the more worrisome part of a strong culture is the ever present possibility of abuse. One of the needs filled by the strong excellent company cultures is the need most of us have for security. We will surrender a great deal to institutions that give us a sense of meaning and, through it, a sense of security. Unfortunately, in seeking security, most people seem all too willing to yield to authority, and in providing meaning through rigidly held beliefs, others are all too willing to exert power. Two frightening experiments, those of Stanley Milgram at Yale and Philip Zimbardo at Stanford, warn us of the danger that lurks in the darker side of our nature. The first, familiar to many, are Stanley Milgram's experiments on obedience. Milgram brought adult subjects off the street into a Yale lab and asked them to participate in experiments in which they were to administer electric shocks to victims. (In fact, they were not doing so. The victims were Milgram conspirators and the electric shock devices were bogus. Moreover, the experimental protocol made it appear that the choice of both the victims and the shocker was random.) Initially, Milgram had the victims placed in one room and the shock givers in another. Following instructions to them by a white-coated experimenter (the authority figure), the shock givers turned the dial, which went from 'mild' to 'extremely dangerous.' On instruction, they administered the electricity, and to Milgram's surprise and disappointment, the experiment 'failed.' All went 'all the way' in administering shock. One hundred percent followed orders, although in earlier written tests over 90 percent predicted they would not administer any shock whatsoever. Milgram added embellishments. He connected the rooms with a window, so the shock givers could see the 'victims' writhe in pain. He added victim 'screams.' Still, 80 percent went to 'intense' on the dial, and 65 percent went to 'extremely dangerous.' Next he made the victims appear to be 'homely, 40-year-old female accountants.' He took the experiments out of the university and conducted them in a dreary downtown loft. He had the shock giver hold the victim's hand on the electric charge plate. All these steps were aimed at breaking down the subject's acceptance of the white-coated experimenter's authority. None worked very well. People still by and large accepted authority. Milgram postulated numerous reasons for the outcome. Was it generic ? That is, is there species-survival value in hierarchy and authority that leads us all to submit ? Are people simply sadistic ? He concluded, most generally, that our culture has failed almost entirely in inculcating internal controls on actions that have their origin in authority. In the other case, Zimbardo advertised in a newspaper in Palo Alto, California (a prototypical upper-class community), soliciting volunteers for a 'prison' experiment. At dawn one Saturday morning he went out, picked the volunteers up, booked them, and took them to a wallboard 'prison' in the basement of the Stanford University psychology building. Within hours of their arrival, the randomly assigned 'guards' started acting like guards and the randomly assigned 'prisoners' started acting like prisoners. Well within the first twenty-four hours, the guards were behaving brutally...both physically and psychologically. By the end of the second day, a couple of the prisoners were on the verge of psychotic breakdown and had to be released from the experiment. 'Warden' Zimbardo, afraid of his own behavior as well as that of the others, stopped the experiment four days into a ten-day protocol. The lessons are applicable to the cultures of excellent companies, but the apparent saving grace of the latter is that theirs are not inwardly focused. The world of the excellent company is especially open to customers, who in turn inject a sense of balance and proportion into an otherwise possibly claustrophobic environment. On the whole, we stand in awe of the cultures that the excellent companies have built. Despite their inherent dangers, these cultures have made their companies unique contributors to society. (Ibid. PP 78-80)

They deduce the riskiness of a firm with strong culture from two cases of extremely limited experiment in setting and participant characteristics. They concluded that companies with strong culture have excellently contributed to the society while having held their innate risk all the way.

The above argument seems that corporate culture is given to its members from above, and that the members do not participate at all in forming the culture. In reality, however, corporate culture is a gathering of organizational attributes where all its members' modes of viewing, ways of thinking and state of being are collectively reflected.

Taken together, how much it is strong is not an appropriate measure of performance of an organization.

Theory II

The perspective of Theory II asserts that what is of consequence is the content of culture as well as its strength. It further maintains that there is no generally good cultural content nor effective and adaptive culture tailored to any condition. Corporate culture can only be good if it fits in with the things related to it. It is effective when it has adaptability to the conditions of an industry, the segments of industry strategically specified by a firm's strategy, and the business strategy of a firm itself. For instance, fast decision-making and non-bureaucratic conducts would be effective to a firm in the highly competitive environment, but could hurt a company in the traditional life insurance business. Management by hunch and experience would be effective to a small firm, but harmful to a large corporation. The important thing is whether it is strategically appropriate or not.

If the choice of strategies is appropriate for a firm, however, its performance can not be enhanced unless it has norms and values that help it exist in changing conditions. A company with a strategy appropriate to the market can still fail if the strategy does not match the company's culture. Its long-term performance, in such a case, would certainly deteriorate. But, why would it happen ? The answer is 'an entrenched culture can make implementing new and different strategies very difficult'. (J. P. Kotter and J. L. Heskett, 1992 P 41) Once corporate culture is entrenched in a firm, it can not easily be changed strategically.

Let us take up, then, a case of Theory II. R. T. Pascale and A. G. Athos presented a concept of the '7-S model' in their book, *The Art of Japanese Management*. (R. T. Pascale and A. G. Athos, 1981) That model consists of such elements as strategy, structure and systems on the one hand, and those of style, skills, staff and superordinate goals on the other hand. What leads a firm to success is, they think, to build an interdependent and reinforcing network by combining the former elements with the latter ones. The argument goes further : if the network can not be formed in a complete way or there are some conflicts among the elements, corporate performance is bound to be weak. They explain the 7-S model as follows :

The striking differences between Matsushita and ITT lay not so much in the strategy of these two organizations as a whole, for in large part they were quite similar. The distinctions are certainly not a result of the matrix-type organizational structure that was nearly identical in both companies. Nor did the real differences reside in the systems...at least, in the formal hard copy systems, which in each case involved detailed planning and financial reports with a highly operational focus. These first three factors are insufficient to explain the differences we have seen. The real differences lay in the other elements...the management style, the staffing policies, and above all the spiritual or significant values...and, of course, the human skills to manage all of these. It might help to visualize at this point the seven elements we have been using to understand better both Matsushita and ITT. (Ibid. PP 79-80)

The seven elements are summarized as follows.

THE SEVEN S's

Strategy	:	Plan or course of action leading to the allocation of a firm's scarce resources, over time, to reach identified goals.
Structure	:	Characterization of the organization chart (i.e., functional, decentralized, etc.)
Systems	:	Proceduralized reports and routinized processes such as meeting formats.
Staff	:	'Demographic' description of important personnel categories within the firm (i.e., engineers, entrepreneurs, MBAs, etc.). 'Staff' is not meant in line-staff terms.
Style	:	Characterization of how key managers behave in achieving the organization's goals ; also the cultural style of organization.
Skills	:	Distinctive capabilities of key personnel or the firm as a whole.
Superordinate Goals	:	The significant meanings or guiding concepts that an organization imbues in its members.

(Ibid. P 81)

Let's review briefly what the terms mean. Strategy pertains to a firm's plan of action that causes it to allocate its scarce resources over time to get from where it is to where it wants to go. Structure refers to the way a firm is organized...whether it's decentralized or centralized, whether it emphasizes line or staff...in short, how the 'boxes' are arranged. Systems refers to how information moves around within the organization. Some systems are 'hard copy' types...computer printouts and other ink on paper formats that are used to keep track of what's going on. Other systems are more informal...like meetings. These three elements ... strategy, structure, and systems...are probably quite familiar to most readers. The other four factors are what we call the 'soft' S's.   Staff pertains not to staff in the line/staff sense, but to demographic characteristics of the people who live in an organization. Are they 'engineering types,' 'used car salesman', 'MBAs', 'computer jocks' ?   Skills refers to those things which the organization and its key personnel do particularly well ... the distinctive abilities that truly set them apart from competition. For example, as an organization Procter & Gamble is skilled at marketing ; its management is skilled at sustaining the institution's vitality and maintaining an environment that continually provides new, viable consumer products to replace older ones. It should be noted that skills apply on both the organizational and interpersonal level. ....Two final factors require definition. Style refers to the patterns of behavior of the top executive and the senior management team. For example, Geneen and his team had a tough, facts-oriented style. Style also refers to that of the organization as a whole. Clearly, Matsushita has a different style from ITT. Superordinate goals (which include the spiritual or significant meanings and shared values of the people within an organization) refer to the overarching purposes to which an organization and its members dedicate themselves. These are rarely bottom-line secular goals like growing x percent a year or obtaining y percent return on investment. Rather, this factor pertains to values or goals that 'move men's hearts' and that genuinely knit together individual and organizational purposes. (Ibid. PP 80-82)

R. T. Pascale and A. G. Athos call the group of elements of staff, skills, style and superordinate goals the soft S's. What is characteristic of the soft S's is that the crux of that group is corporate culture as seen in the elements of style and superordinate goals. On the other hand, the hard S's are composed of strategy, structure and systems. The core of the group is apparently strategy, while structure and systems are rather auxiliary. To put it simply, therefore, the 7-S model is basically a concept of two elements that there is strategy on the one hand and corporate culture on the other hand.

They further extend their argument on the 'hard' elements and the 'soft' ones.

As noted earlier, American managers tend to overfocus on the 'hard' elements. In part this may stem from the attention academics have paid to these same variables. Some of the best work done in business schools in recent decades has been in advancing our understanding of the 'cold triangle' of strategy, structure and systems. Each one and the relationships among the three are particularly susceptible to analytical, quantitative, logical, and systematic investigation. In short, 'science' of one kind or another, rigorous observation and conceptualization... thinking, if you prefer...were required. That's what business schools value. That's how professors get rewarded. And that's what fits our culture's central beliefs about managing. It's no surprise that such an approach dominates curricula in business schools. Of course, there were some all along who 'felt' this was 'all wrong'. They advanced the case of the four 'soft' elements in various ways, and with varying degrees of success. But, as is often the pattern in our culture, this group saw their interests as an 'either' to the dominant group's 'or'. The 'tough-minded' disdained the 'soft-hearted' ('unscientific' was their most restrained abuse) ; the latter somewhat less confidently disparaged the former ('inhuman' was a favorite epithet). Each tended to act as if their own preference was central, the other's peripheral. Each seemed to believe God was on their side. It seemed for a while that each was driving the other to further extremes. The tiresomely pedantic intellectual techniques ultimately developed by one group rivaled the undisciplined, anti-intellectual, emotionally excessive 'experiences' of the other. This dichotomization recently has softened. But in the meantime a generation of managers has been educated in apparently opposed camps, and too few have managed their own successful synthesis. Most stayed in the 'hard-headed' camp, as that was what corporations clearly rewarded (if one was not too obvious about it). The few who went with the other side ended up in one or another 'nurturant' roles. Whether formally in Personnel or not, they made a great show of whatever quantitative support they could muster for their cause. Far more important, we think, than the unwitting contributions of academics to our dilemma, and the unfortunate criteria by which corporations reward their graduates, is the fact that our culture itself impedes the kind of synthesis the Japanese manage so well. These US cultural givens include some central assumptions and perceptions about :

1   The nature of the human condition, in particular those conditions of ambiguity, uncertainty, and imperfection which must be addressed by managers.

71

2   The nature of human beings, in particular the split between the person as object (i.e., interchangeable unit of production) and the person as subject (i.e., the unique, whole human being) within the corporation.

3   The nature of relationships, in particular in reference to issues of dependence and independence in corporate life.

4   The nature of leadership, in particular those behavioral skills and patterns of behavior which encourage others to identify with corporate goals.

5   The nature of significant or spiritual meanings, in particular those beliefs which guide behavior within companies and give meaning beyond exchange of time and effort for money and power.

One can see clearly the great difference between Mr. Matsushita and Mr. Geneen in the ways they 'thought' about human beings in reference to the subject/object dichotomy. Geneen seemed to regard other people as objects to be used to achieve his purpose, while Matsushita seemed to regard them as both objects to be used and subjects to be honored in achieving his and their purposes. When Geneen found an executive wanting, the man was humiliated or fired. When Matsushita made a similar discovery, the man's group was marked as ineffective and he was reassigned, even demoted, and the opportunity for the individual to grow from the experience was stressed. These are very different approaches indeed. But the Japanese way makes possible great corporations that successfully persist in harmony with their culture's deepest values. The American way often does not. And the problems that result eventually make our largest companies less competitive and effective, eventually candidates for government help or protection, or petitioners in bankruptcy courts. In short, the four 'soft' elements can no longer be regarded as frosting on the corporate cake. They are indispensable parts of any corporate commitment to long-term success. (Ibid. PP 82-84)

R. T. Pascale and A. G. Athos have stated that while the hard S's, the core of which is strategy, are fundamental and of essence in doing business, the soft S's, the crux of which is corporate culture, are significant ingredients as well in attaining a long-term success. That is, within the framework of a strategy, they think, it is of consequence to make corporate culture effective enough to gain a good long-term performance.

They will next argue on the relationship between strategy and superordinate goals, i.e., corporate culture.

An organization's superordinate goals emerge, in part, from leadership which instills values through clarity and obsessive focus. A firm's history also contributes to its enduring value system. Organizations tend to grow through stages, face and surmount crises, and along the way learn lessons and draw morals that shape values and future actions. Usually these developments influence assumptions and the way people behave. Often key episodes are recounted in 'war stories' that convey lessons about the firm's origins and transformations in dramatic form. Eventually, this lore provides a consistent background for action. New members are exposed to the common history and acquire insight into some of the subtle aspects of their company. Matsushita made a considerable effort to pass on his company's legacy to each new recruit. Superordinate goals are immensely helpful at the beginning of a strategic era. Setting out to build a fast-food empire, not only did McDonald's stress price, quality, profit, and market share, but they believed they were performing a real service to Americans living on limited means. This 'social mission' gave a larger meaning to operational objectives. The cooks and order takers in McDonald's franchises found higher-order goals helpful in accepting the company's rigorous quality control system. Strict standards could be met more readily when seen in the context of 'helping society'. As one manager put it, 'The lower down you go in an organization, the more difficult it is for employees to identify with the firm's business objectives. A firm's social and humanitarian objectives are far more tangible to a dishwasher or janitor than is its goal of market share.' Toward the end of a strategic era, a firm's past meanings can get in the way. In fact, this invisible force has undone late-in-an-era executives who sought to change things. Case studies of incumbents whose terms of office spanned the time periods when their organizations were moving from one era to another seem to indicate that they 'failed' more often than they 'succeeded.' Organizational meanings can be so deeply ingrained, so fundamental to what people think and feel, and so important to their beliefs about their jobs and themselves, that when initially these meanings are challenged, there is often resistance and later dismay and a great sense of loss. One recent example is the current transition at AT&T. That company's deeper meanings were built on providing reliable and inexpensive telephone service to America. The firm's superordinate goal uniting managers, workers, and even stockholders has been the 'social mission' of providing a reliable, low-cost phone system to America. Bell Labs and Western Electric further enshrined AT&T's pride as the 'World's Best Telephone Company.' But in the early 1970s competitive data processing applications began to spill over into AT&T's traditional domain. It became increasingly clear that the telecommunications fields and computer fields were overlapping. The

73

result: AT&T was increasingly facing competitors in the computer industry; it would have to broaden its focus, change its strategy and become more of a marketing-oriented company in order to meet that competition. Ideally, its superordinate goal needed to shift to being a 'marketer and innovator in telecommunications.' In competing with firms like IBM, AT&T has to tailor its products and respond more rapidly to shifting market needs ... in short, to make significant changes in all Seven S's. Two of AT&T's chief executive officers saw this happening and began to move to change the company's direction. Their names are not likely to be enshrined as 'great leaders' in AT&T's legends. They attempted to realign the strategy, but all of AT&T's systems were oriented toward tight operational controls ... the sort that keep track of costs, operator errors and equipment reliability in the traditional phone service. They also encountered a staff of employees whose middle and senior managers had come up through the ranks as managers of telephone switching offices and repair facilities. With backgrounds in engineering and accounting, this management cadre lacked strong instincts for sales and marketing. In short, there were formidable barriers to change. Perhaps this helps us understand why the current chairman of AT&T believes that the shift to a true marketing orientation will require twenty years. Transitional times are periods in which older meanings and behaviors are slowly and painfully relinquished, and leaders who anticipate future threat when things are still apparently going well make an important contribution that is not often widely recognized at the time or, for that matter, honored later. Not until this painful and difficult process has run its course will the readiness for new meanings permit a 'great leader' to articulate them convincingly. Strategic eras impose their own destiny on organizations and their leaders. (Ibid. 195-197)

As stated above, what is needed in achieving a firm's best performance is to work out the most appropriate strategy under a given circumstance and at a given time, and to change the contents of the firm's conventional culture overall to suit that strategy. It is the work of business leaders, they think, that makes corporate culture congruous with strategy.

The reality is, however, that a deeply imbedded corporate culture is too formidable a barrier to overcome for a strategy to be successfully implemented. No explanation is given, here, of how to address such a barrier. It is the modes of viewing, ways of thinking and state of being of the constituents of a firm that form and support its corporate culture. The members of a firm have a significant and integral stake in the corporate culture. Their stake is, however, altogether neglected here.

Theory III

The Theory III is that only a corporate culture which helps its organization predict and adapt itself to environmental change can be associated with excellent performance in the long run. The environment-adaptive culture legitimately appraise and encourage entrepreneurship. It will make it easy, therefore, for people to find out and exploit new opportunities. It puts emphasis on leadership. The primary function of leadership is to make change. So, if leadership activities would prevail throughout an organization, it could give rise to active risk-taking, productive dialogue, motivation and other traits necessary for the growth of the firm. On the other hand, an organization with an unadaptive culture tends to be bureaucratic and reactionary, averting risks, and not to be creative. Information can not flow in a quick and simple way through that kind of organization. Since control is broadly emphasized, people grow less motivated and less enthusiastic about work.

In the adaptive culture, on the contrary, there are such organizational traits as leadership, entrepreneurship, prudent risk-taking, candid discussion, innovation, flexibility, and focus on customers' importance. The traits above are thought to lead a firm to attain excellent performance in an environment where change is the rule of the day. Among the traits above, leadership is the key. J. P. Kotter and J. L. Heskett says,

> In the firms with more adaptive cultures, the cultural ideal is that managers throughout the hierarchy should provide leadership to initiate change in strategies and tactics whenever necessary to satisfy the legitimate interests of not just stockholders, or customers, or employees, but all three. (J. P. Kotter and J. L. Heskett, 1992   P 50)

In a culture adaptive to environmental reality, the norms of conduct is directed by the value system which puts a premium on the legitimate needs of stockholders, customers and employees. It is also people initiating change and its methods that are emphasized here.

Theory IV

Among the theories briefly explained so far, Theory III on corporate culture and performance seems to be the most convincing. However, that theory, too, has weaknesses on the following three points.

The first is the relationship between corporate culture and

competitiveness. When one says that a certain corporate culture brings about a good performance, one presupposes that there is competitiveness duly interposed between corporate culture and performance. As was accounted for in Chapter 7, firms have their own structure of competitiveness, respectively, which is composed of various competitive elements. The relationship between those elements and corporate culture is of the utmost importance in analyzing a long-term economic performance. Theory III does not take into account that relationship.

The second is the relationship between organizational traits and corporate culture. It is quite certain that organizational traits like leadership, entrepreneurship, prudent risk-taking, flexibility and so forth are significant in doing business under all the circumstances. But, what cultural attributes give rise to those traits ? What modes of viewing things, what ways of thinking, and what state of being are recognized behind the organizational traits ? Theory III neglects them.

The third is the criteria of deciding what values to be preserved. Although it is said that the needs of stockholders, customers and employees should be respected, and that people initiating change is highly valued, no criteria is put forth for the preservation of values. What values to be preserved is to be judged in the context of a firm's competitiveness structure. Whether a firm's culture is healthy or not is also to be checked out in accordance with the Three-Layer Structure of Enterprise Competitiveness.

Then, what is the author's view on corporate culture and performance ?

In the first place, in his view, there is generally good cultural content suited to every condition. That content is healthy and adaptive, including things of value to be preserved. In the second place, it is firmly associated with the elements of the competitiveness structure. That is, a culture that fits in well with the Three-Layer Structure of Enterprise Competitiveness can create superior performance in the long run. The author calls that view the 'Theory IV'. It is the people of a firm that backs up its competitiveness structure. They have, respectively, their own modes of viewing, ways of thinking and state of being, which are collectively reflected in the firm's competitiveness structure. A company is a living being. It has the personality of its own. How does such a living being with its own personality build up competitiveness ? That is, again, the main theme of the book. The linkage between corporate culture and competitiveness is the key to uncovering the relationship between corporate culture and performance.

76

9   Ohmi Merchants

Here, we present a model typical of Japanese corporate culture, i.e., the corporate culture of Ohmi Merchants. The Ohmi Merchants are an archetype of Japanese business concern, where many firms today have their origin. During the Tokugawa times (1603-1867), they established a nation-wide distribution network and invented an accounting system which matched well, indeed, that of bookkeeping in the West at that time. After Meiji Restoration in 1868, they made all their efforts to found a textile industry, trading concerns and others, and ever since have contributed greatly to the development of Japanese economy. (E. Ogura, 1990)

Why did many merchants spring out of the land of Ohmi ?   And why have they kept their solid business foundation to this day ?

In the Tokugawa period, Japan was a feudal society.   Naturally, feudal lords had a great influence over their domains. They certainly recognized the importance of merchants and their business activities, but only to the extent that the merchants contributed to the self-sufficient economy of their domain. But for that, they made a number of regulations in a law form or others curbing merchants' activities. That is, the economy at that time was basically of autarky within a feudal domain. Protectionism and a managed economy generally prevailed in those circumstances. However, some lords had such domains that were not one single area but composed of many areas. Among them there were lands of small size yet geographically distant from the main part of their domains. Those distant lands were usually left loosely administered. They hardly exercised, in reality, their policies of protectionism and managed economy over those undersized areas since they were too far removed from their main domains. If they had done that, indeed, it would have rendered them overextending themselves and hurting their main domain economy. The land of Ohmi where a number of merchants sprang out was a gathering of such diminutive lands. (E.Ogura, 1990)

Geographically advantaged, people of Ohmi were full of the ethos of freedom. People from different origins came to be merchants there. At first, they started out as a local merchant, doing business deals with industries in Ohmi, and then expanded nation-wide. They broadly peddled the goods manufactured by the local industries outward to the east and to the west of the nation, while, on the way back, they brought back things available only in the regions they visited. Then, they built bases for business and concluded partnership with other merchants all through the country, thus, forming a nation-wide distribution network.

It is said that their distribution network in the Tokugawa times was literally a leading one the world over in ingenuity and effectiveness. Take the case of Kimono, for instance. People in Kyoto traditionally put a great value on costume. Kimono was usually called by the name of its production region. That is, they had Isezaki, or they had Tango, and so forth. They properly used various Kimono from different regions for different purposes. The Kimonos came from many regions, including Kyoto, eastern Japan (Isezaki, Kiryu, Ashikaga), central Japan near the Japan Sea (Echigo), north of Kyoto (Tango), and on the Pacific side in central Japan (Okazaki). People in Kyoto, in that way, enjoyed wearing many kinds of Kimono produced in different regions, which was made possible not only by the distribution network, but also the division of work nation-wide at that time. Ohmi Merchants' activities across feudal domains, therefore, deserve to be praised in creating and promoting such a nation-wide distribution network and division of work. The feudal domain economy could not have possibly accomplished that. It was nurtured and established by the free enterprise activities by Ohmi Merchants.

Now, let us next look into the modes of viewing things and the ways of thinking characteristic of Ohmi Merchants. Ryoyou Nakai was one of the typical merchants in Ohmi and the founder of the House of Nakai, a big and well-established merchant house at that time. He valued money-making and the accumulation of wealth in a right way and believed in the legitimacy of profit-making. He, on the other hand, admonished his successors and followers that a merchant is to live a long and healthy life, keep savings, be diligent, and not to fall into luxury. He did not believe that any business opportunity comes right out of fortune. It seemed to him, moreover, that use of calculation, business talent, credit and the like are needed for business, but the crux of business is the balance in decision making. It is due to a merchant's intention and efforts whether he can attain such a balance during his lifetime. Yet, to be truly the excellent merchant house, he thought, it would need a man of good will after another who succeeds his merchant house through generations. R. Nakai and his successors alike made a number of contributions and donations to the public good. The contributions are, in fact, too numerous to mention. They put the primary importance on men of integrity in their view of values.

As a general way of doing business, Ohmi Merchants made it a principle to sell volume at a small profit. That principle was associated with their saving-minded and diligent way of life. Even with a minimal rate of profit, the return on capital could be sufficiently increased if sales turned over many times. To increase the rate of sales, they tried hard to find as many customers as possible, and be diligent enough to keep other merchants from taking their customers. That is the way they performed business activities.

There were, of course, various merchants in this period other than Ohmi Merchants. Among them, Bunzaemon Kinokuniya and Mozaemon Naraya were the most well-known. In the Tokugawa times, people in Yedo, the capital city of Japan at that time, enjoyed eating mandarin oranges, usually on the first 7 days of a new year. The mandarin oranges were mostly transported by vessel in advance from Kishu located almost in the middle of Japan. One year, however, there arrived typhoon just when Kishu merchants began transporting mandarin oranges to Yedo by ship. No merchant, therefore, dared to risk taking them to Yedo except one, Bunzaemon Kinokuniya. His vessel, full of oranges, plowed through that violent stormy weather, and by good fortune reached Yedo. He built great wealth, and later became a timber wholesaler under the shogunate patronage. On the other hand, Mozaemon Naraya was also a timber wholesaler. He took a chance to make a fortune when there occurred a destructive fire in Yedo in the last half of the 17th century. Later, he conspired with government officials to make undue profits on his business.

The way of doing business followed by both B. Kinokuniya and M. Naraya was that of a speculator. In addition, they always associated themselves with persons in power, sought protection from them in one way or another. Therefore, it could be said that they are the exact opposite of Ohmi Merchants. Due to their moral misconducts, they lost public confidence, and came to be looked down upon by the public. Thus, the House of Kinokuniya eventually deteriorated and collapsed during his lifetime, while the House of Naraya went out of existence in his successor's time.

Ohmi Merchants did not concern themselves with any speculation at all. They were concerned with how effectively and balanced they could perform business.

In that context, the merchants in Ohmi had ingenious accounting systems. Take an accounting system devised by the House of Nakai for instance. Through their system, interestingly enough, one can reach the same settlement of accounts as to be obtained when following the modern double entry book-keeping although the methods of keeping and adjusting accounts differ altogether. The accounting system of Nakai was put in practice in 1753, and it could well match the German integrated book-keeping system which was in practical use in the last half of the 18th century. (E. Ogura, 1990)   That system, furthermore, was a decentralized as well as concentrated management accounting system so that it could be used as a means of both managing branch offices and working out a consolidated statement of settlement. It was a highly advanced system attesting to their genuine pursuit of economic rationality.

Next, at the core of their ethics were the 'Ancestors'. They believed the house succeeded from its ancestors, with its prosperity to be credited to them, and that the descendants could only make a return with a blessing from their ancestors through diligent work. They may have felt that the ancestors watched them all the time.

Along with the Ancestors, they also had the 'Public' in their mind. Business is for the Public. The results of business are to be credited to the Public. And so forth. In other words, they put the same importance on the public as on their ancestors. Yet, they felt no contradiction between the Ancestors and the Public, which was very much characteristic of their practical ethics.

As for education, they had their own way. Girls who wished to be a merchant's wife usually went into the domestic service of a merchant family as a maid to learn manners. They underwent practical training in the merchant's private house, and acquired the know-how to respond quickly and properly in all the circumstances. Applicants for a business house, on the other hand, went through an elementary education provided by the merchant's wife at her private house. Depending on the grades they received, they were assigned to a post in the business house. Although a merchant's wife was not in the business house, she had information on its employees sufficient to evaluate them from a different angle than its employer, i.e., her husband.   Thus, the employees could be educated and treated as fairly as possible.

Ohmi Merchants possessed a variety of traits necessary for the success of business like those mentioned above. Under the feudal system, in this context, it is only natural that there was opposition to their modes of viewing things, their ways of thinking and state of being.

A Confucian scholar, Tozan Ro, was an advisor to the lord of Sendai located to the northeast of the country. There remains a report of his to the lord that is typical of such an opposition. In the 1754 report, he commented that many Ohmi merchants came to the domain of Date, freely peddling and selling things on credit. He severely criticized such behavior in view of Confucian thought.

One of the core principles of Confucianism is classicism, i.e., a logic of regulation. That view is, indeed, totally dissident from the free, broad-minded way of thinking of Yaoyorozu-No-Kami characteristic of Ohmi Merchants.

Confucianism also preaches that a man of virtue is not to be a man of expertise and skill. It looks down upon experts, skilled people and the like, and disrespects techniques and technology. It is not concerned with rational activities at all. The man of virtuous principle is, thus, altogether dissimilar to the Ohmi Merchant's ways of Kanjyo and Shugo which are, respectively, to absorb new things and to combine things of different character.

Another characteristic of Confucian thought is to respect family-oriented homogeneity. It refuses heterogeneity of any nature, which unduly impedes the creation of new ideas, ingenious contrivance or invention. Ohmi Merchants' Musubi characteristic is exactly the opposite to the family-oriented homogeneity. In selecting the successor of their house, for instance, Ohmi Merchants have their own criteria that a successor is to be a man of ability and a man of good will. With generation after generation of succession of their house in mind, they chose the right person as a successor among their employees including their children, or sometimes from outside. They were concerned with an ever-going and ever-creating enterprise, i.e., making and forming on a continual basis. That is why most of them have kept such a solid foundation of business to this day. The Confucian scholars could not have possibly imagined such a long succession of business by merchants in Ohmi.

Now, let us finally classify Ohmi Merchants' modes of viewing, ways of thinking and state of being explained thus far in accordance with the Three-Layer Structure of Enterprise Competitiveness.

In Enterprise Logistics, at first, there is the ethos of freedom in Ohmi. As mentioned previously, the land of Ohmi was a gathering of diminutive lands which belonged to the feudal lords who settled, across other lords' territory, in their far-distanced main domains. Primarily due to such logistic reasons, therefore, those small lands in Ohmi were out of self-sufficient policies and controls exercised by the owner lords. Geographically advantaged, people in Ohmi started out as local merchants, conducting business dealings with industries in Ohmi, and then expanded their business around the country. Naturally enough, enterprise ethos flourished in the land of Ohmi, which was further promoted by success after success of Ohmi Merchants. The enterprise ethos was, in turn, backed up and strengthened by the integrity recognized among successful merchants in Ohmi. To be truly the excellent merchant house, they thought, a man of good will is needed through generations. It is apparent, here, that Akaki-Kokoro, an attribute of Japanese culture, lived in their mind. Yet, everyone living in Ohmi could have been a merchant, whether he was a farmer, a craftsman or a samurai by origin. People were all Yaoyorozu-No-Kami.

Next, Ohmi Merchants concerned themselves with no speculation at all. The right way of doing business, they thought, is to work hard with sweat on one's brow and form something new or of value. It certainly agrees with the mind of Musubi. In selecting their successor, furthermore, they had their own criteria that a successor is to be a man of ability and a man of good will. What they were concerned with is how they could maintain their standards through many generations. Its longevity and healthiness, i.e., making and forming on a continual basis, was their main concern, which is also an expression of the mind of Musubi.

Ohmi Merchants admonished that one ought to live a long and healthy life, keep savings, be diligent, and not to fall into luxurious habits. Value of Cleanliness and Hajio-Shiru-Kokoro seemed to be expressed here in their own way.

In Enterprise Economic Base, secondly, Ohmi Merchants excelled at creating their infrastructure. They established bases for business around the country and widely conducted partnerships with other merchants all over to form a delicate, nation-wide distribution network. Thus, products manufactured locally were broadly and smoothly distributed to every corner of the country. One can recognize here Kanjyo way of thinking (take in new or useful things).

The economy of a feudal society was, in itself, of a feudal domain-based self-sufficiency. It was Ohmi Merchants' nation-wide activities that allowed communication among people and information on different products to diffuse to all corners of the country. The diffusion of information was, in turn, facilitated by the power of Kotodama among Ohmi Merchants.

In Management System, thirdly, their way of doing business was, as already stated, to sell volume at a small profit. They did not settle in vested rights, which is characteristic of Yaoyorozu-No-Kami, since they were well aware that their business became increasingly competitive, requiring cost-cutting measures and the like. They tried to increase opportunities to see as many people as possible in selling their goods, and be diligent enough for other merchants not to be able to catch up.

As for Ethics, there was the 'Ancestors' in the crux of their ethical norms. The house or its capital was handed down from generation to generation. The prosperity of business was due to the blessings given by them. Descendants can only make a return for such a blessing through diligent work. That way of thinking represents a shame-sensitive mind, i.e., Hajio-Shiru-Kokoro, to ancestors.

Along with the 'Ancestors', there was 'the Public' in the mind of Ohmi Merchants. Yet, they felt no contradiction between the Ancestors and the Public. They were kept in good balance. To put it another way, there was a tense balance held between money-making and ethical norms. In every respect, they thought that the crux of business was to perform with balance. That is the essence of a healthy enterprise. Such a state of being is characteristic of Many Deities as One Deity, One Deity as Many Deities. They placed much emphasis on how to best attain a balance in their way of business.

To sum up, let us show the competitiveness elements and the cultural attributes of Ohmi Merchants' in a table form as follows.

Table 9.1   Competitiveness elements and cultural attributes of Ohmi Merchants'

I   Enterprise Logistics
  • Enterprise ethos
    Ethos of freedom.   Yaoyorozu-No-Kami

    Integrity.   Akaki-Kokoro
  • Provision of norms
    No concern with speculation.
    Criteria for the selection of   Musubi
    successor.
  • Enterprise ethics
    A long and healthy life.
    Keeping savings.   Value of Cleanliness

    Prohibiting luxury.   Hajio-Shiru-Kokoro

    Diligence.

II   Enterprise Economic Base
  • Infrastructure
    A nation-wide distribution network.
    Taking in whatever things of value.   Kanjyo
  • Diffusion of new ideas, planning
    and others
    Activating communication.
    Diffusion of information on   Kotodama
    products.

III Management System
  A. Effectiveness
    Not settling in vested rights.   Yaoyorozu-No-Kami

B. Tense balance between effectiveness
   and ethics
   Ancestors and the Public.

Tense balance between money-making and ethical norms.	Many Deities as One Deity, One Deity as Many Deities
The crux of business being how balanced a way it is performed.	

C. Ethics

Making a return for blessing of Ancestors.	Hajio-Shiru-Kokoro

We can see from the table a clear competitiveness structure in Ohmi Merchants' way of business. Due to this, most of their businesses have been kept on to this day in an unbroken succession. We can also find, here, their cultural attributes that are highly adaptive to that structure of competitiveness. In other words, the modes of viewing, the ways of thinking and the state of being of Ohmi Merchants are rightfully and collectively reflected in their competitiveness structure, which forms the personality of Ohmi Merchants, i.e., Ohmi Merchants' culture in its own way.

10 The theory of Baigan Ishida's on merchant way

While Ohmi Merchants were typical of merchants in the Tokugawa times, there were a number of other merchants similar to the Ohmi in the merchant way. That is, many merchants in that period had the same modes of viewing, ways of thinking and state of being as duly recognized in the merchants in Ohmi. Baigan Ishida precisely noticed these common views, ways of thinking and state of being among the merchants and organized them in thought.

Baigan Ishida's idea was based on the Kami Way's modes of viewing, ways of thinking and state of being, and it was developed further to become a fundamental theory that guided merchant activities. Thus, his idea had an influence on a great many merchants in the Tokugawa period. His theory, named the 'Learning of Human Nature', had been disseminated throughout the country and became a great force in thought by the last half of the 18th century. His view corresponded well to what the merchants had encountered, experienced and thought in their practical business, and thus greatly appealed to them.

Baigan Ishida was originally a manager of a merchant house in Kyoto. His writings, *Tohi Mondo* (Questions and Answers between City People and Country People) and *Seika Ron* (How to Administer A Merchant House), were written particularly for merchants. His followers, who had periodically listened to his lectures, were mostly merchants in Kyoto and Ohmi with some samurai. Baigan Ishida's view was known as the Learning of Human Nature where the main theme was economic rationality and merchants' ethics.

Here, therefore, we shall set forth Baigan Ishida's theory, which underlies the thought of Ohmi Merchants, an archetype of Japanese corporate culture.

Apprenticeship

Baigan Ishida was born as the second son of a land-owned farmer in a mountainous region not far away from the city center of Kyoto in 1685. When he became 11 years old, he went into service as an apprentice in a Kyoto merchant house. At that time, it was customary that those after the first son enter into apprenticeships either at a craftsman's or a merchant house if the farm land was not big enough to cultivate. The first son only stayed with the farmland to succeed his father's job. At the age of 20, however, Ishida resigned from his job at the merchant house and came back to his parents to assist them in their work in the field and in the mountains. After having spent 3 years with his family, he again went into service at another merchant house, called the House of Kuroyanagi, which was much bigger than the previous one and located in the northern part of Kyoto city. (M. Shibata, 1962)

Interest in the Kami Way

From the beginning of his service at the House of Kuroyanagi, his intention was to diffuse his views about the Kami Way to other people. According to the *Jiseki* (Baigan Ishida's Achievements) written by his followers later on, he had been keenly anxious to advise people of the way of human nature, i.e., the Kami Way. In fact, he said in the opening statement of his book *Seika Ron* written after retirement of his service, 'If no one is willing to listen to my thought, I would even stand at the corner of a town to convey what I have in mind to people'. (M. Shibata, 1956)   Here, we can see his expression of Kotodama in that he would like to diffuse his thought to as many people as possible.

While he was in service at the merchant house, he did not really intend to be a merchant. In peddling around in the southern part of Kyoto city, he always had some books with him and tried to read them whenever time permitted. He got up earlier in the morning than his colleagues to read books by his room's windows. Late into the night, after his colleagues went to sleep, he would enjoy reading. Yet, he worked hard for the merchant house in the daytime. It is duly thought, therefore, that reading these books as a youth formed the basis for his later theories.

At the age of 23, to repeat, Baigan Ishida came out of the mountainous region back in Interior Kyoto to serve the merchant house of Kuroyanagi. Then, all of a sudden, he had an enthusiastic desire to disseminate his thought on the Kami Way. The Kami Way was, to him, to be the way of human nature and to be a model universally accepted for men's conduct. He is said to have enthusiastically advised the house owner's mother, who deeply believed in Buddhism, of his thought on the Kami Way. On hearing that, an elder clerk in the house expressed bitter complaints about him to her, but the old woman told him that Baigan's willingness to learn the Kami Way was very serious and genuine and so that it would be better to leave be. It is thought that such an open and generous ethos as prevailed in the House of Kuroyanagi was conducive to his mental development during his youth.

His thought on the Kami Way, in that context, is considered not to have belonged to any school of thought like Yoshida Shinto, but to have originated in the popular modes of viewing and ways of thinking of the Kami Way shared among the public. He organized those viewing and ways of thinking into his own way of thought. Yet, his motive to build his thought was highly ethical. It was to advise people of the way of human nature. That is, the thought of the Kami Way that he had diligently studied from his early days was not that transmitted from a teacher to a disciple, but a popular thought on the Kami Way generally prevailed among people at that time. He developed it into a systematic thought of his own. (M. Shibata, 1962)

His sincere intention to pursue and attain the essence of genuine human nature and be the model for human conduct himself had been strengthened while he was engaged in business activities at the merchant house, having encountered people of various kinds and things of diverse nature through business dealings.

The central idea of Baigan Ishida's learning

The central subject of the Learning of Human Nature is how to know human nature. To recognize human nature is not the same as to observe things in an ordinary way and distinguish their merits and demerits. It is also different from reading a book to understand the meanings in it. In those ordinary knowledge, there is an observer and things to be observed which are pitted against each other. In recognizing human nature, an observer and an object to be observed are to be unified. It is usually the case, in that context, that one often sees himself as an object in exploring what he has in mind. He would mostly take that kind of self-examination as knowing human nature. To truly understand human nature, however, one has to go beyond the self-examination and attain the unity of his self with the object. Here, we can see a mental framework of 'Many Deities as One Deity, One Deity as Many Deities', a characteristic attribute of the Kami Way. That is, a conceptual framework of the identity of one with many is obviously expressed.

Often, one might say, 'I don't understand myself'. In this case, the person doesn't know himself or herself because the mind is in a disintegrated state due to internal and external diverse forces where wants and desires are pitted against reflection so that one is not in a position to make a decision and take a course of action. When one is devoted to work, on the contrary, he or she would have no doubt nor fear, and thus, the mind can act as it wishes. The latter case is very close to the state of recognizing human nature since one (he or she) is unified with many (himself or herself). Baigan Ishida took such a state as above knowing human nature.

At the age of 35 or 36, Baigan Ishida encountered Ryoun Oguri, a man of thought, which provided him a keen incentive to further develop his ideas. Ryoun Oguri seemed to have considered him to be his sole successor. When he fell into illness and at last came to close to death, therefore, he called Baigan and told him that he would give him the whole set of books with his own notes. Baigan Ishida, however, turned it down frankly and said that he did not want to receive them. When Ryoun Oguri asked the reason, Baigan Ishida is said to have answered that he would set forth his own ideas when the time came. He could not have agreed to the Confucian ideal that one is to pay respect to one's teacher on all matters and that one is to keep things as they are.

Baigan Ishida's learning was not such knowledge that could be transferred from a teacher to a disciple as a bottle of water is poured into another bottle. Everyone has to get himself to the bottom of a matter at any price and create his own thought to cope with it. That is the mind of Musubi in the Kami Way, i.e., making and forming things new, that was the base of Baigan Ishida's learning.

Beginning lectures

At the age of around 42, Baigan Ishida resigned his post as manager at the House of Kuroyanagi, and then, when he became 45 years old, he began to spread his ideas to the public. He settled in a corner of a Kyoto city street to start his lectures. His intention was that everyone could freely listen to him with no letter of introduction and no fee whatsoever. His way of anti-authoritarianism and egalitarianism were obviously reflected here. That is, there is a way of thinking expressed that people, who attend his lectures, are all Yaoyorozu-No-Kami. In the beginning period, the reputation of his lectures was well spoken of by some, but ill spoken of by others. It seemed to be rather natural since he was only from a manager of merchant house by origin, taught himself without a teacher of renowned status or scholar title, and started delivering lectures with no particular patronage.

Texts used for his lectures were of diverse kinds, including even books on Confucianism and Buddhism, and yet he interpreted those books in his own way, which was squarely in contrast to the classicism and annotationism of the Confucian thought. For instance, in one of his chief writings, *Tohi Mondo* (Questions and Answers between City People and Country People), he quoted many words and clauses from books on Shinto, Buddhism, Confucianism and others to use them fragment by fragment as means to express his thought with no consideration of their original connotations whatsoever. (M. Shibata, 1962) We can see, here, his own way of thought is that one is to take in what-ever kind of book if it is useful and beneficial, particularly in curing people's weakening mind. This, in turn, is very much cha-racteristic of Kanjyo and Shugo in the Kami Way.

Initiative

Baigan Isida thought that the ultimate end of learning has little to do with literal abilities. Writings of any nature are only instrumental in getting to know one's mind. If one is so much concerned with letters and expressions that he is likely to forget his final aim, he ought not to read books. The truth lies in the daily practices and thought of a person's life. Therefore, a person is to endeavor to attain his real self, i.e., the truth, at any cost, for himself.

Baigan Ishida thus regarded initiative as of primary significance in people's daily life, which is rightfully a manifestation of the thought of Yaoyorozu-No-Kami.

Daily morning task and lecture

He usually awoke early at dawn, washed his hands, opened the doors and cleaned up the rooms of his house. Then, having made a light in a miniature shrine, he worshipped the Sun Deity, the Deity of Furnace, Community Deities in his native place, prayed to Confucious, Amitabha and Shakyamuni in Buddhism, and did reverence to his teachers, ancestors and father and mother. Following that, he had breakfast, and after having finished it, he rinsed out his mouth and took a rest for a while. Then, his lecture began. His followers described Baigan Ishida's daily practice like the above later on in their writings, *Jiseki* (Baigan Ishida's Achievements).

To wash one's hands and to clean the rooms of his are symbolic of Misogi in the Kami Way. While praying to a variety of deities, Confucious, Buddha and others as a whole reveals a view that they are

90

all Yaoyorozu-No-Kami. Saints of any nature are considered to be part of Yaoyorozu-No-Kami. There is not one absolute being in the Kami Way.

In the lectures he delivered, daily and actual matters of life were often taken up as the main subject. His approach to the real problems was diverse from case to case so that it would be difficult to summarize his general solutions to them. However, the most appropriate approach to many different problems in life, in his case, comes down to how one can discard one's egos to be honest and stand to reason. That is, he encouraged his listeners to respect Value of Cleanliness, following Akaki-Kokoro.

For instance, a case among the questions and answers between him and listeners was this (M. Shibata, 1956) :

> Question : 'There is a person who entered a family as an adopted son. If his father by blood killed his foster father, should he revenge himself upon his father by blood for a wrong ?'
>
> Answer : 'Yes, he should take revenge for his foster father's death, and carry the head of his deceased father by blood to a place of requiem'.

Here is stated a way of righteousness to follow which has nothing to do with blood relationship.

The theory of Baigan Ishida's

He taught how to get to the bottom of human nature through learning. It was broadly known as the Learning of Human Nature in later years. It is a theory mostly centered on practical ethics where he put emphasis not on knowledge of things per se, but on the linkage of knowledge with deed, i.e., practical learning.

It is also characteristic of his theory that merchants are regarded as significant members of a society, playing a due role for it. It seemed to him that the four social classes in the Tokugawa period (samurai, farmer, craftsman and merchant) were basically not different in rank, but in profession. The samurai, farmer, craftsman and merchant were a part to be played by each in the whole society. Here is a view that people are all Yaoyorozu-No-Kami. He thought that a merchant's role is to streamline the flow of products by changing things in excess into those lacking. (M. Shibata, 1956)   A profit earned in business dealings is thought to be a right reward for a merchant's activities. 'It is a merchant way to gain a due profit'. (M. Shibata, 1956) Economic rationality is put in perspective here.

Baigan Ishida severely protested the fixed idea that prevailed particularly in the samurai class at that time that a merchant was only pursuing his own earnings, but not for the cause of any social justice. According to his theory, the right merchant way is to serve people in the society who are the true master of wealth. Therefore, it is a wrong way for a merchant to collect businesses of sweet poison, unduly gain double earnings and thus put an end to his merchant life. Value of Cleanliness is apparently placed, here, as one of the fundamental principles in the merchant way.

Honesty

One who does not doubly collect a profit is a man of honesty. A honest man, as Baigan Ishida puts it, is the one who is to perform his duty in the right way and come back into the genuine state of his being. That is, a genuinely honest man is certain to hold Akaki-Kokoro. In January 1743, in this connection, the following question was raised at a regular monthly meeting of Baigan Ishida's from one of his followers. (M. Shibata, 1956)

> A merchant's three big customers were so damaged by a flood in northeastern part of the country last summer that he could not collect any accounts receivable from them. He has not been able to pay, therefore, any penny of his loan himself up to this New Year's Day. How should he do with it ?

To that question, Baigan Ishida answered.

> The merchant ought to sell out all his belongings with nothing left to clear off his debts. Then, people would be impressed with it and not leave him alone. If his life is likely to be poor, he could live in peace with an honest mind of Deity throughout his life.

Here is expressed a way of thinking that 'Deity dwells in an honest man's heart'. His writings, *Tohi Mondo*, like the above, mostly centers on the matter of merchant way. 'What I do is to teach merchants that there is the right merchant way for them'. (M. Shibata, 1956) His close followers were, in reality, all but merchants from Kyoto and Ohmi.

Saving and Diligence

While Baigan Ishida explains saving and diligence in detail in the Learning of Human Nature, most thoughtful merchants at that time were well aware of the necessity and meaning of saving and diligence through their experience and reflection on them. What Baigan Ishida did, therefore, is to get such merchants' experience and reflection into the thought of his and conceptualize and set them in order. Yet, the crux of the concepts in his thought was Akaki-Kokoro and Value of Cleanliness. He put the views of saving that generally prevailed among people into a right perspective in his book *Seika Ron*. That is, he united saving with the Value of Cleanliness in thought and explained that the saving is not to store money per se but the means in making people's life affluent by distributing money all around the society and vitalizing its economy. That indicates that the stored money is to be effectively used as a new investment. His thought on saving is, therefore, of ethical stoicism founded on economic rationalism. (M. Shibata, 1962) He said,

> When I talk about saving, I also mean that one is to restore honesty, a genuine human nature...Everyone is a son of Heaven. An individual each is a miniature cosmos. There is, therefore, originally no ego in him. (M. Shibata, 1956)

It is egalitarian and a way of Yaoyorozu-No-Kami to say that everyone is a son of Heaven. People are respectively a cosmos and thus their ego is not of original nature. That is, Akaki-Kokoro is their original state of being.

Learning of Human Nature

Baigan Ishida passed away at the age of 60 in 1744. It is Choan Tejima (1718-1786), the youngest follower of his that assumed and developed further the Learning of Human Nature. Choan Tejima was an owner of a wealthy merchant house in Kyoto. In 1735, when he was 18 years old, he became one of the followers at Baigan Ishida's and at the age of 28 lost his master by death. In 1761, he resigned from his post in the house and began to disseminate the Learning of Human Nature. He, at first, inaugurated a school named the Goraku-sha, and then, opened three schools, i.e., Shusei, Jishu and Meirin. The Learning of Human Nature was thus broadly diffused all over the country and at the end of the 18th century it had become a great force in thought in the society.

As set forth before, Baigan Ishida's theory expressed, succinctly and clearly, the most representative merchant way in the Tokugawa period. Furthermore, its basic modes of viewing, ways of thinking and state of being have succeeded in an unbroken succession to this day and become basic to the right merchant way. There are values here to be preserved beyond the times and an abundance of contents closely connected to the Three-Layer Structure of Enterprise Competitiveness.

11 Corporate culture of today

In Chapter 9, we have explained the culture of Ohmi Merchants, an archetype of Japanese corporate culture, which was duly observed in their ways of doing business. Their business performance was based on a firm and solid competitiveness structure which was formed and supported by their modes of viewing, ways of thinking and state of being, i.e., their corporate culture. Ohmi Merchants' culture was, indeed, remarkably adaptive to the Three-Layer Structure of Enterprise Competitiveness.

Now, let us next here take up the US and Japanese firms of today, and shed light on their corporate cultures.

11.1   Healthy culture of Hewlett-Packard's

Hewlett-Packard was founded by two Stanford University electrical engineers, Bill Hewlett and Dave Packard, in 1939. They started out with their business in a leased garage in Palo Alto, California. In the 1940s and the 1950s, Hewlett, Packard and their colleagues developed a philosophy fundamental to business and ways of operations, which was later known as 'the HP way'.

The crux of the HP way lies in the view that a firm is to serve everyone, who has a stake in the business, with integrity and fairness. With that marked core of business thought, the HP way means and stresses the following. (Kotter and Heskett, 1992)

1   To recognize employees' individual achievements and offer them opportunities to upgrade their skills and abilities.
2   To show employees trust and respect.
3   To provide the firm's customers products and services of the greatest value.
4   To have genuine interest in arriving at effective solutions to the customer's problems.
5   To make profit a high priority.

6   To be a very good corporate citizen.
7   To give a priority to initiative and creativity.
8   To give a priority to managers who engender enthusiasm and teamwork throughout the organization.
9   Management-by-wandering-around.
10   Informal collegial behavior.
11   Some form of management-by-objectives.
12   An avoidance of layoffs.
13   To minimize acquisitions.
14   Not to buy market share.
15   To create an open-architecture office structure.
16   To create fully integrated and autonomous operating units.
17   To create a minimum of bureaucracy.
18   To create comfortable work environments.

Bill Hewlett and Dave Packard were firmly convinced that the HP way was indispensable and conducive to their business success.

In the 1970s and the 1980s, its adaptability to changes was tested. The changes during those periods had been more fundamental in nature than at any time in the firm's history. The life cycles were, indeed, all but over for some of the main products. They had to bring out new products, and face increased competition, sluggish markets, and other difficulties. The result was that they went through that exceedingly difficult and adverse environment successfully. The key to the success was ascribed to the core philosophy and values recognized in the HP way.

Into the 1990s, they encountered a crisis. Surprisingly enough, they were also capable well to cope with drastic changes in the market as well as within the organization.

In this context, a study on Hewlett-Packard UK was conducted in the aftermath of that crisis, i.e., during January to March 1994 by P. McGovern and V. Hope-Hailey. The study was :

> Part of a five year research project which was commissioned by a consortium of fourteen major British-based firms who are collectively known as the Leading Edge Forum Ltd. This project examines human resource strategies, policies and procedures and their implementation by senior, line and general managers. A particular focus of the research is the relationship between the informal organization and human resource management in practice. (P. McGovern and V. Hope-Hailey, 1996.)

The study was carried out with both semi-structured interviews and a questionnaire survey. Out of the total 36 interviews held, 12 were conducted with middle managers from the Computer Systems Organization using a methodology called 'The Unwritten Rules of the Gamme' which was developed by Peter Scott-Morgan at the A. D. Little consultancy, another sponsor of the research. In the questionnaire survey, a total of 400 questionnaires were randomly distributed to employees at the head office. Out of them, 215 questionnaires were returned for a response rate of 56%.

In 1992, in the wake of the economic downturn, Hewlett-Packard faced with difficult decisions on downsizing. Senior management, then, endeavored to remind staff of the business performance and the management-by-objectives that the company has historically emphasized, while they exercised the voluntary severance programme. That program was the first one the company had ever adopted. One of the longtimers said, 'HP has hardened up a lot. It's difficult to have core values when you are getting rid of people. There is an underlying nervousness. We're O.K. but who knows tomorrow.' (Ibid. P 18) Another longtimer said, 'HP is like any other company when the chips are down. We needed the doze of realism. You can't have that (The HP way) unless you bring in revenue'. (Ibid. P 18) In spite of some critical remarks like the above, however, the senior management succeeded in convincing people as a whole of the company's emphasis on business performance and management-by-objectives, particularly, in a crisis. In 1993, Hewlett-Packard UK increased its turnover by 43%, generating profits of $ 85 million compared with a break-even position in 1992. (Ibid.)

A number of factors contributed to that turnaround including favorable market changes, new product launches and cost-cutting measures. The most dramatic change, among others, was found in the organization structure, with the voluntary severance programme being part of it. The company decided to return to a decentralized structure that would give freedom back to its individual business units. The result was, expectedly, impressive. On the other hand, it seems natural that there were some scars left in the organization after the redundancies.

> Among the 'scars' left in the organization was a reduction in the number of promotion possibilities on the managerial ladder. Promotion would now be more infrequent and involve greater increases in responsibility than before. Managers also had to deal with wider spans of control in the new structure which meant that larger numbers of staff now reported directly to them. (Ibid. P 19)

What is to be noted, however, is that HP staff retain a high level of commitment to the organization despite the reduction in the number of managerial ladder. P. G. McGovern and V. Hope-Hailey said,

> This was most clearly expressed in the survey evidence on organizational commitment. In comparison to the other organizations which participated in this research, the summary indicator for organizational commitment in Hewlett-Packard, 4.6, was significantly higher than for any of the other organizations ranging from 3.4 down to 2.4. Furthermore, HP's managers did not have a lower level of organizational commitment than non-managerial staff even though it was primarily management jobs which were made redundant. (Ibid. P 19-20)

On the other hand,

> Employees also expressed positive views on the people-oriented culture of the organization in the course of the interviews. While many of them acknowledged that they had doubts, or that it would never be quite the same after the recent upheaval, they still judged HP to be a 'damn good place to work'. (Ibid. P 20)

Not a few people, furthermore, thought that the HP way's values were congruous to their own.

Thus, P. G. McGovern and V. Hope-Hailey concluded, 'it would appear that HP has weathered the crisis with most of its culture and traditions intact, at least, for those who remain with the company'. (Ibid. P 21)   The corporate culture of Hewlett-Packard seems to be as healthy as ever. It is still indispensable and conducive to their business as the founders expected.

Then, how is the HP way, which have been through such a severe trial, associated with the Three-Layer Structure of Enterprise Competitiveness ? And how is it put in perspective with the US culture ?   Let us first see how the thought and core values of the HP way, listed from (1) to (18) at the beginning of this section, fit in with the three layers of Competitiveness Structure, i.e., I. Enterprise Logistics, II. Enterprise Economic Base, and III. Management System.

In Enterprise Logistics, to begin with, there is a way of thinking that one is to give a priority to initiative and creativity (7), which must have been an Enterprise ethos since the foundation of the firm. A priority is also given to managers who engender enthusiasm and teamwork throughout the organization (8). Those managers are supposed to be conducive to Enhancement of initiative. It is the company's basic principle to minimize acquisitions and not to buy market share (14). Preparation of investment conditions is, thus, kept in order. As previously noted, the crux of the HP way is to serve everyone, who has a stake in the business, with integrity and fairness. Integrity and fairness correspond to Akaki-Kokoro, an attribute of Japanese culture, and likewise forms the core part of Enterprise ethos.

In Enterprise Economic Base, secondly, it is stressed that one is to be a very good corporate citizen (6). Cooperation with and participation in a community fall into the category of Environmental improvement and conservation. Looking inward to the firm, on the other hand, to create a comfortable work environment (18) is emphasized to be properly considered in attaining Improvement of the physical environment of workplace.

It is significant, next, that the management positively communicate with their staff. Management-by-wandering-around (9) is a good means in promoting Diffusion of new ideas, planning and others. By creating an open-architecture office structure (15), furthermore, such an atmosphere is to be fostered that one can get in and out of office freely, and contact to communicate with others smoothly. The open-architecture office structure, in that sense, conduces to Diffusion of new ideas, planning and others.

In Management System, thirdly, there are stressed to render profit a high priority (5) and to have a principle of management-by-objectives (11), both of which are in pursuit of Effectiveness. By improving cost, quality and delivery terms simultaneously, in that context, a firm can provide its customers products and services of the greatest value (3). On the other hand, the company intends to recognize employees' individual achievements and offer them opportunities to upgrade their skills and abilities (1). In other words, it is committed to the development of personnel's abilities, which falls into the category of B. Tense balance between effectiveness and ethics. The principle of creating fully integrated and autonomous operating units (16) is, in turn, associated with Organizing techniques. Informal collegial behavior (10) and a minimum of bureaucracy (17) are indicative of a flat organization with few rungs in the managerial ladder. It is emphasized, next, to have close relationship with customers such that the company is willing to have genuine interest in arriving at effective solutions to the customers' problems (4). An avoidance of layoffs (12) is usually taken to confirm long-term employment guarantee. Finally, in Ethics of Management System, showing trust and respect to employees (2) is listed as one of the core values. It is, interestingly, congruent with the way of thinking that every member is a leading actor, which is characteristic of Yaoyorozu-No-Kami, an attribute of Japanese culture.

Taken together, the HP way is evidently adaptive to the Three-Layer Structure of Enterprise Competitiveness. It is quite certain that its core philosophy and values are universally acknowledged and accepted. It would be applicable everywhere.

Now, let us secondly look into how it is put in perspective with the attributes of US culture. The HP way is certain to be associated with Individualism, an attribute of the US culture, as shown in the following thought and core values.

(1) To recognize employees' individual achievements and offer them opportunities to upgrade their skills and abilities.

(2) To show employees trust and respect.

(6) To be a very good corporate citizen.

(12) An avoidance of layoffs.

(17) To create a minimum of bureaucracy.

An avoidance of layoffs is listed here in the context of individual dignity. In other words, employees are individually respected and therefore their layoffs are to be avoided as much as possible. The HP way also embodies the cultural attributes of Competition as the following.

(3) To provide the firm's customers products and services of the greatest value.

(5) To make profit a high priority.

The above two principles seem to be expressed with all the time competitive market in mind.

Taking Things Easy, another attribute of the US culture, can be recognized in (9), (10) and (15).

(9) Management by wandering around.

(10) Informal collegial behavior.

(15) To create an open-architecture office structure.

Out of the above three, (9) and (15) fall into the category of Diffusion of new ideas, planning and others as stated previously. One can see how the attribute of Taking Things Easy allows communication between managers and staff to be activated. Diligence, another US cultural attribute, is manifested in the following principles.

(4) To have genuine interest in arriving at effective solutions to the customer's problems.

(13) To minimize acquisitions.

(14) Not to buy market share.

Out of the above, (13) and (14) remind us of Protestant ethics which have contributed greatly to economic performance in the US.

As for Youngness, Newness and Future-orientedness, which are particularly characteristic of US culture, the following two are thought to represent them.

(7)　To give a priority to initiative and creativity.

(8)　To give a priority to managers who engender enthusiasm and teamwork throughout the organization.

The attributes above are the principles needed vitally for a firm to keep its youngness and newness and develop its business with orientation towards the future.

Finally, as to the Concept of Precise Time, another cultural attribute, it is recognized in (11).

(11) Some form of management-by-objectives.

In carrying out things, preciseness and speed are important.

To sum up, the competitiveness elements and the cultural attributes of the HP way are shown in a table form as follows.

Table 11.1   Competitiveness elements and cultural attributes of Hewlett-Packard's

I   Enterprise Logistics
   ·   Enterprise ethos
       To serve everyone who has   Individualism
       a stake in the business with
       integrity and fairness.
       To give a priority to initiative   Youngness and
       and creativity.   Newness, Future-
                                            orientedness

   ·   Enhancement of initiative
       To give a priority to managers   Youngness and
       who engender enthusiasm and   Newness, Future-
       teamwork throughout the   orientedness
       organization.
   ·   Preparation of investment conditions
       To minimize acquisitions.   Diligence
       Not to buy market share.   Diligence
   ·   Enterprise ethics
       To serve everyone who has   Individualism
       a stake in the business with
       integrity and fairness.

II   Enterprise Economic Base
   ·   Environment improvement and
       conservation
       To be a very good corporate citizen. Individualism
       To create comfortable work
       environments.
   ·   Diffusion of new ideas, planning and
       others
       Management by wandering around.   Taking Things
                                             Easy
       To create an open-architecture   Taking Things
       office structure.   Easy

III   Management System
   A. Effectiveness
       To provide the firm's customers   Competitiveness
       products and services of the
       greatest value.

To make profit a high priority.	Competitiveness
Some form of	Concept of
management-by-objectives.	Precise Time
B. Tense balance between effectiveness and ethics	
To recognize employees' individual achievements and offer them opportunities to upgrade their skills and abilities.	Individualism
To have genuine interest in arriving at effective solutions to the customers' problems.	Diligence
Informal collegial behavior.	Taking Things Easy
To create fully integrated and autonomous operating units.	
To create a minimum of bureaucracy.	Individualism
An avoidance of layoffs.	Individualism
C. Ethics	
To show employees trust and respect.	Individualism

As was explained in Chapter 8, Section 1, there is generally a good cultural content however the environmental conditions change. That content is healthy, adaptive to change, and holds values to be preserved. It also fits in well with the elements in the Three-Layer Structure of Enterprise Competitiveness. Hewlett-Packard is typical of the organization with such a culture. Its people's modes of viewing, ways of thinking and state of being are collectively reflected in the HP's competitiveness structure, while they form a personality of their own, i.e., a corporate culture called the HP way.

11.2 Unhealthy culture of Xerox's

Let us next address a firm of unhealthy culture as opposed to a firm with healthy culture. A company we take up here is Xerox. In the 1950s, Xerox had an excellent, healthy corporate culture as noticed in the principles put forth by the then president Joe Wilson.

His principles are said to have been 'faith in people, concern for customers, and economic power through innovation, marketing, patents, and worldwide presence'. The concern for customers is a theme that emerges again and again in material describing the 1945-65 period. (J. P. Kotter and J. L. Heskett, 1992   P 76)

Into the 1960s and the early 1970s, however, managers were inclined to think in an arrogant way. In 1968, they acquired a small computer company named Scientific Data Systems for 90 times its earnings, and attempted to fling down a challenge to IBM although it was strategically harmful to their other lines of business. On the other hand, their concern for customers weakened badly. Their way of purchasing market share by M&A (mergers and acquisitions) allowed the administration in Washington to bring a suit against them. Their concern for stockholders and costs were also weakened. Issues of turf became a major concern among the management. Managers were further and further intolerant of the initiatives and leadership from people in lower ranks. Decision-making was centralized as well. Managers were absorbed in running a business by the numbers and ceased to be good communicators with the staff. In 1973 and 1974 when a task force presented some proposals to the management, they altogether neglected them. When a line of personal computers was invented at Palo Alto Research Center, the executives at that time decided not to exploit that opportunity. In 1975, furthermore, when such Japanese companies as Canon, Minolta, Ricoh and Sharp started introducing copiers broadly into the market, Xerox was too slow in coping with them. Primarily due to that delay, 'its worldwide share of copier revenues fell from 82 percent in 1976 to 41 percent in 1982. It also failed completely to adapt to the requirements of the computer industry'. (J. P. Kotter and J. L. Heskett, 1992   P 77)

From 1983 onwards, Xerox has endeavored to redirect itself to an organization with a healthy culture. However, there is a long way to go. There seems to be many weaknesses to overcome.

To put the elements of weakness in perspective, therefore, we shall, here, put in order how Xerox in the 1970s was inappropriate to the Three-Layer Structure of Enterprise Competitiveness.

In Enterprise Logistics, to begin with, there was an arrogant way of thinking among the management which eventually led them to neglect the enterprise ethos established in the early days of the firm. Managers were absorbed in running a business by the numbers. There was, therefore, no such atmosphere where every member is willing to grapple with any situation without hesitation and without worrying about failure. That is not adaptive to Enterprise ethos. Next, the fact that issues of turf became a major concern among managers is indicative of lack of teamwork among personnel. In addition, managers became intolerant of the initiatives and leadership from ranks. Personnel, accordingly, must have lost pride and confidence in upholding their enterprise's competitiveness as well as a sense of representing their enterprise. That, in turn, would have exerted an adverse impact on diligence and positive activities of the personnel, which is squarely at odds with Enhancement of initiative. In addition, an anti-monopoly suit was brought to Xerox, which is opposed to Provision of norms. As to investment, the firm purchased Scientific Data Systems for 90 times its earnings to acquire market share. It is inappropriate to Preparation of investment conditions.

In Enterprise Economic Base, secondly, there was a problem associated with Diffusion of new ideas, planning and others. Managers were only concerned with figures, and they were not a good communicator any more. A decision-making was centralized as well. So, new ideas, reform, improvement and intelligence on new products were not diffused smoothly within the organization.

In Management System, finally, there was a problem that the management's interest in stockholders and costs weakened to a noticeable degree. They also became little conscious of the effectiveness of their business and their relationship with customers. They decided not to utilize the line of personal computers invented at Palo Alto Research Center, and thus lost a good chance to enter into a computer business. Under the circumstances that proposals from employees were not paid attention to, there was no view that every member was a leading actor.

To sum up, the elements at Xerox, which were inappropriate to the Three-Layer Structure of Enterprise Competitiveness, are classified in a table form as follows.

Table 11.2   Elements at Xerox inappropriate to the Three-Layer Structure of Enterprise Competitiveness

I   Enterprise Logistics
  · Enterprise ethos
    To deteriorate enterprise ethos   Inappropriate
    established in the early days of
    the firm.
    No such atmosphere where every   Inappropriate
    member is willing to grapple with
    any situation without hesitation
    and without worrying about failure.
  · Enhancement of initiative
    Lack of teamwork among personnel.   Inappropriate
    Personnel's loss of pride and   Inappropriate
    confidence in upholding their
    enterprise's competitiveness as
    well as a sense of representing
    their enterprise.
  · Provision of norms
    An anti-monopoly suit brought   Inappropriate
    by the government.
  · Preparation of investment conditions
    To purchase a firm to acquire market   Inappropriate
    share.

II   Enterprise Economic Base
  · Diffusion of new ideas, planning
    and others
    Managers are only concerned with   Inappropriate
    figures, not a good communicator.
    New ideas, reform, improvement and   Inappropriate
    intelligence on new products are not
    diffused smoothly within the
    organization.

III Management System
  A. Effectiveness
    The management's interest in   Inappropriate
    stockholders and costs weaken.
    The management are little conscious   Inappropriate
    of effectiveness.

B. Tense balance between effectiveness
and ethics
The management are little conscious   Inappropriate
of their relationship with customers.
C. Ethics
No such a way of thinking that   Inappropriate
every member is a leading actor.

Now, let us next see how Xerox's cultural content is incongruent
with the US culture. To begin with, in such an atmosphere that no one
is willing to grapple with any situation without hesitation and without
worrying about failure, there is no place for Youngness, Newness and
Future-orientedness, three attributes of the US culture, to exist.
Individualism is not recognized since there is no view that every
member is a leading actor ; since the personnel lose pride and
confidence in upholding their enterprise's competitiveness as well as a
sense of representing their enterprise.

Next, it is opposed to Diligence to purchase a firm only to acquire
market share. There is, furthermore, no indication of the sign of Taking
Things Easy as a decision-making is centralized ; as managers are only
concerned with figures, and so not a good communicator. Finally, there
is the management's neglect of Competition in that their interest in
stockholders and costs weaken ; and in that they are little conscious of
effectiveness.

Taken together, thus, Xerox in the 1970s was typical of the firm
with unhealthy culture.

As was stated earlier, Xerox has endeavored from 1983 onward and
still endeavors to get back on a path to a healthy corporate culture.
There seems to be a long way to go. However, as is exemplified in
Nissan's case in the next section, it would not be impossible to turn it
around.

11.3 Turnaround of Nissan's from unhealthy culture

We shall introduce here a firm that has attempted a turnaround from its
unhealthy culture. The firm we take up is Nissan.

In the 1970s, Nissan enjoyed a growth stage in its postwar history.
As is often the case, the firm added layer after layer of management to
the structure of its organization during the growth period. Due to that
over-layered structure, problems of an imminent nature or matters of

significance could not possibly reach top management quickly and effectively enough. It is under these circumstances that Yutaka Kume was appointed president of the firm. It was in 1985. He first decided to form a task force of 13 middle managers from Nissan Technical Center in collaboration with an outside consulting firm, McKinsey & Company, to transform the NTC drastically. The task force, in turn, made suggestions and proposals which seemed to be appropriate to change it in the right direction.

According to their proposals, in the first place, the NTC introduced an organizational change into its R&D department in 1986. As a result, R&D general managers, who had tended to be inward-looking, were put concurrently into three market-oriented groups.

Next, simultaneous engineering was introduced. To reduce design time and improve quality, it was required that each department passes on information to all the other departments at the earliest possible time. Simultaneous diffusion of information was thus encouraged throughout the organization.

Thirdly, the choice of uniforms was left up to the staff. It was thought that freedom of dress and expression would add to creativity and innovation in their work as stylists and designers.

In the fourth place, to further promote the creative atmosphere, a flex time system was introduced in which people were only required to be at the center from 10:30 to 15:30. Accordingly, they had more leeway in how they used these time. In the fifth place, to enhance awareness of competitors, the design staff were permitted to own a competitor's car. It was a breakaway from the conventional thought that people coming to the center ought to drive Nissan's car.

In December 1986 after the measures above had been taken, Kume put forth a statement of corporate philosophy to all Nissan employees. He emphasized four principles in it which J. P. Kotter and J. L. Heskett quoted as follows.

> We must keep in touch with the global market, creating attractive products through our innovative and reliable technology..... We must be sensitive to customers' needs and offer them maximum satisfaction based on steadfast sincerity and ceaseless efforts to meet their requirements.... We must focus on global trends, making the world the stage for our activities, and to nurture a strong company that will grow with the times....We must foster the development of an active and vital group of people who are ready and willing at all times to take on the challenge of achieving new goals. (J. P. Kotter and J. L. Heskett, 1992 P 129)

Kume personally carried the message of that statement to the employees of the factories or offices he visited. It was unprecedented for a Nissan's president.

Through the changes thus far described at Nissan, the first product that appeared on the market was the Silvia, called the 240sx in the US. Before having launched the development of Silvia, in that context, there had been a failure of Skyline in 1985 and a fiscal loss in 1986. Managers had gradually recognized that the difficulties set before them could not be possibly overcome by their conventional methods or ways of thinking. Under those circumstances, it seems natural that they had reached a consensus opinion that the Silvia project was to be committed only to young employees. The average age of members who participated in the project was 28. The members discussed what the project was to be and collectively made decisions about it without any interference of top management. The Silvia, a sporty compact coupe, was targeted at twenty-five-year-olds. An outside fashion designer was invited, furthermore, to help determining the style of the car.

The form of decentralized decision-making taken on the Silvia project represented a break from tradition in Nissan's centralized bureaucracy. Before the launch of the project, indeed, the case was not rare that an executive came and asked for some change, for instance, in the headlights of a car since it did not suit his taste. One of the project members remarked,

> These last minute changes no longer occur. With the old culture, subordinates were always looking at those above them in the hierarchy. No matter the content of the issue, they would just say, 'yes' to whatever they were told to do. (Ibid. P 134)

The break from the old practice was reinforced by Kume himself. He backed away from selecting the final model of Silvia. He just looked at the two clay models, and went off, saying nothing.

The Silvia was the first product that was not only designed but sold by young staff. One of them said,

> What was unique with the Silvia was that discussing sales promotion in the meetings, we did not have to have the presence of older managers. All of us younger employees could get together and discuss freely what we thought about the car. All we had to do was to report the results to our manager. So we were free to say whatever we thought. These discussion sessions led to new ideas. (Ibid. P 134)

109

After the debut of Silvia, the project members were also engaged in sales activities at the dealership. They directly touched the market and perceived its response.

As is known well, the Silvia made a great hit, which indicated a sign of Nissan's turnaround.

Now, then, let us see how Nissan's transformation elements fit in well with the Three-Layer Structure of Enterprise Competitiveness, and how they are congruent with the attributes of Japanese leading culture.

Many elements may be related to Enterprise Logistics. These include that the Silvia project was committed only to young employees ; that the decision-making was left in the charge of young employees ; that the top management executed a break from tradition in Nissan's centralized bureaucracy. Those elements represent an effort to recover the enterprise ethos founded in the early days of the firm. That endeavor means to perform Yomigaeri, i.e., reviving to get a new life.

Their transformation includes that the choice of uniforms was left to the staff. It is intended that the freedom of dress and expression is given back to the staff and let them freely exchange their views and opinions. In other words, it aims to appeal to Musubi among the staff. To further promote the atmosphere of creativity, i.e., of Musubi, a flex time system was introduced, which is conducive to Enhancement of initiative in that it helps increase pride and confidence in employees' own work. In the meetings of sales promotion on the Silvia, there was no presence of older managers, which facilitated the atmosphere that the young members freely expressed what they thought without any hesitance.

In Enterprise Economic Base, secondly, there was the introduction of simultaneous engineering. To reduce design time and increase quality, each department at NTC was required to transfer information to all the other departments at their earliest time possible. Simultaneous diffusion of information was thus promoted.

It is mentioned, next, that Kume, president of the firm, carried himself his message on corporate philosophy to the employees. No previous president did it that way. Here, we can find Kotodama, a cultural attribute representing Diffusion of new ideas, planning and others. Speed and smoothness of communication is a most decisive element among others in Enterprise Economic Base.

In Management System, finally, it is noted that R&D general managers were put concurrently into market-oriented groups. The market is literally 'the Public', i.e., Yaoyorozu-No-Kami. How could the firm attract them ? It is expected to come up with a product that the market truly demands. What the firm is to do first, therefore, is to listen to Yaoyorozu-No-Kami, which may be the primary reason that the general managers were placed in the market-oriented groups. The design staff were, in this context, permitted to own a competitor's car to heighten concern for competitors. It is intended for them to know 'the Public', while encouraging competitive spirit among them. It is particularly emphasized, here, that people have a firm stake in the market.

An outside fashion designer was invited, moreover, to help with the model of Silvia, which is indicative of Kanjyo, a way of thinking that one should absorb whatever things new and of value from outside. It is a good way to introduce new ideas and innovative technologies from outside.

Finally, the fact that the Silvia project was wholly committed to young staff could be ascribed to the thought that every member is a leading actor. Since the project organization had no complicated managerial ladder, the members individually could act much more freely, which may be rightfully called the Yaoyorozu-No-Kami way. They must have felt pride and confidence in their work in such an open atmosphere.

Taken together, let us show Nissan's transformation elements and their corresponding healthy cultural attributes in a table form as follows.

Table 11.3   Transformation elements and healthy cultural attributes at Nissan

I   Enterprise Logistics
   · Enterprise ethos
     Silvia project was wholly   Yomigaeri
     committed to young staff.
     A break from the centralized   Yomigaeri
     bureaucracy.
     Choice of uniforms left to   Musubi
     the staff ; freedom of dress
     and expression.
     No presence of older managers   Musubi
     in the meeting ; free expression
     with no hesitance.
   · Enhancement of initiative
     A flex time system ; adding to
     pride and confidence in one's
     work.

II   Enterprise Economic Base
   · Diffusion of new ideas, planning
     and others
     Introduction of simultaneous   Kotodama
     engineering ; simultaneous
     diffusion of information.
     President personally carrying   Kotodama
     his message over to employees.

III Management System
   A. Effectiveness
     R&D general managers put   Yaoyorozu-
     into market-oriented groups ;   No-Kami
     to listen to the market.
     Design staff permitted to   Yaoyorozu-
     own a competitive car ;   No-Kami
     to heighten concern for
     competition.
     An outside fashion designer   Kanjyo
     introduced ; introducing
     ideas and technologies from
     outside.

B. Tense balance between effectiveness
and ethics
A project organization with
no complicated managerial
ladder ; members little
conscious of organizational
stratum.
C. Ethics
Development of Silvia   Yaoyorozu-
only by young employees ;   No-Kami
every member is a leading
actor.

As was described above, there are now many elements found
contributing to healthy culture at Nissan. It is to be noted, however,
that a healthy corporate culture can only be maintained through
incessant efforts. If it is left altogether inattentive, it is likely to change,
be weak, and deteriorate in one way or another.

As J. P. Kotter and J. L. Heskett stated in their book, *Corporate
Culture and Performance*, the total time required for a complete
turnaround is 5 years in the shortest, and 15 years in the longest. It is to
that extent that corporate culture has to do with business performance.

11.4 Confucianist Company

Confucianist Company, a pseudonym, is a firm with unhealthy
corporate culture in Japan. The company has four main characteristics
in its modes of viewing things, ways of thinking and state of being.
The first characteristic is its paying a great regard to social stratum.
The second is a rule-by-virtue principle, the third is classicism and the
fourth is family-circle homogeneity.

The regard for social stratum is manifested, at first, in its seniority
system. Age and career record are highly respected so that they are the
main criteria in determining the promotion of personnel. It is regarded
as a good deed for one to respect his senior and follow his instructions
faithfully. In meetings, whether held regularly or not, the order of
taking seats among attendants is usually set in accordance with age and
career. There is an atmosphere, indeed, in those meetings that young
people are not to be too forward. Under those circumstances, they are
inclined to take a wait-and-see attitude. They would not dare to plunge

into discussion on whatever subject, and wait and see what move the others make, and then decide how to express their opinion. It seems that young people are not willing to create their own work. Words of despair could only be heard as this : 'It will be useless to express your opinion. It will not go down with them'.

The rule-by-virtue principle, next, is based on a way of thinking that a man of virtue is the right person to instruct people, and that he is more than law in his abilities. According to that principle, a firm's social status and rank are fixed when a man of social eminence assumes the top position at the firm. With the status and rank fixed, the firm is to set up a managerial ladder of ranks in an orderly manner. In an organization thus established with such a managerial ladder of ranks, the atmosphere is so rigid and formal that one could hardly talk to his superior at eye level. Whenever he talks to his superior, he stands while the other sits in a chair. A person standing to talk is at a disadvantage while the other sitting in a chair maintains a psychological advantage. Since his superior is to be treated as a noble man, he would use a term of respect as needed officially. Under such setting, it is too difficult for them to exchange candid conversation and fully understand each other.

In making a proposal which is to be presented to the board, furthermore, one has to do a painstaking preparatory work to obtain consensus on it. He goes around to explain and convince managers concerned to get their consent. In so doing, he is particularly concerned with the sequence of submitting his report. He pays great regard to the status and rank of each manager to decide who is to be submitted first, who is second and so on. What helps him get managers' agreement, in that context, is a sectional group among graduates of a particular university. If a manager to be contacted is from the same university as his, he would probably get the manager's consent. There is a tendency of forming such a sectional group in the firm, which is an adverse effect of the 'school career principle'. The school career principle would demand in the extreme case that a young staff is to hold the same or similar post in due course as his senior who graduated from the same university. There is a rank-oriented valuing principle, here, where a man's dignity is evaluated by his school career and rank in the organization. If that principle reveals itself in meeting a customer, in fact, the customer must feel uneasy and disgusted by it.

Next, there is a deep-rooted classicism at Confucianist Company. People excessively adore a precedent of success in the early days of the firm. They never try to analyze the causes of its success. They take the successful precedent as a golden rule and stick fast to all its details. As a result, the old rules are fixed and the former methods remain unchanged. To protect those rules and methods, indeed, they have made not a few forbidden clauses in the company's law, regulations of diverse nature, and taboo. In such fettered circumstances, it is not likely that new ideas and proposals come out smoothly. A proposal of improvement on a certain matter may come out, but it must be of a short-term nature. It could not possibly be expected for someone to submit a long-term, useful new investment proposal for future opportunities. Conservative ethos prevail in the organization. People put much emphasis on stability and maintenance of the status quo. They never deliberate on launching new lines of business which are, naturally, of consequence for the future of the firm.

Finally, there is family-circle homogeneity within the firm. Employment is limited to those from some specific universities. They have no thought of hiring people of diverse school careers or backgrounds. As a result, a sectionalism is nurtured based on the preference of particular universities. In their family circle, such people would not be accepted that are critical of and willing to challenge the status quo to create new things. Status quo is regarded highly while anything deviating from the status quo is looked down upon. In starting out with a new line of business, it would be necessary to discard previous approaches, to begin with. The personnel, however, never throw them away. As a conventional practice, they send a summer gift and a year-end gift and the New Year's greetings to their seniors. Their primary concern is, accordingly, how to stick to family-circle ties.

At Confucianist Company with such characteristic attributes above, its performance has abruptly lowered. The firm once occupied 50 percent of market share on the average among its lines of product. Its market share has fallen down and is now around a little less than 10 percent on the average. Return on capital is all but zero. Customers' loyalty to the firm's products has fallen off drastically. The company has reached the stage that it could not recover itself without a genuine metamorphosis from its unhealthy culture. Yet, it would take a long time to transform itself in a real sense.

To sum up, we shall put in order the characteristic attributes of Confucianist Company which are inappropriate to the Three-Layer Structure of Enterprise Competitiveness in a table form as follows.

Table 11.4   Characteristic attributes of Confucianist Company

I   Enterprise Logistics
  · Enterprise ethos
    Conservative ethos prevails.
    Too much emphasis on stability and   Inappropriate
    maintenance of the status quo.
    Quite a few regulations and taboo.   Inappropriate
    Common sense taken too high.   Inappropriate
    Not to accept those willing to   Inappropriate
    destruct the status quo.
  · Enhancement of initiative
    A wait-and-see attitude ;   Inappropriate
    not willing to create one's
    own work.
  · Preparation of investment conditions
    A long-term, useful new investment   Inappropriate
    proposal can not be expected.

II   Enterprise Economic Base
  · Diffusion of new ideas, planning
    and others
    Too difficult for managers and staff   Inappropriate
    to exchange candid conversation.

III Management System
  A. Effectiveness
    Old rules and former methods   Inappropriate
    remain unchanged.
  B. Tense balance between effectiveness
    and ethics
    Not a few forbidden clauses ;   Inappropriate
    alternatives are minimal.
    The firm's managerial ladder of   Inappropriate
    ranks firmly established ;
    many-layered structure.
    Fixed sequence of submitting   Inappropriate
    one's report ; no capacity to
    cope with things flexibly.

C. Ethics

Age and career respected high ; appropriate transfer of personnel is curbed.	Inappropriate
A sectionalism based on the preference of a specific university ; not fair employment.	Inappropriate
Evaluation of personnel by school career and rank ; no just and fair promotion of personnel.	Inappropriate
A practice of sending gifts to one's seniors.	Inappropriate

Confucianism is not the mainstream of Japanese culture. Its remnant, however, still remains. It surely exercises an adverse effect on the competitiveness of a firm and drives its performance down. E. Muramatsu calls that adverse effect the 'Poison of Confucianism'. Business leaders would be recommended to find and eradicate that poison before it gets deep inside the organization and does harm.

12 Competitiveness and corporate culture

A good company is one with good and healthy modes of viewing things, ways of thinking and state of being. A bad company is one with bad and unhealthy modes of viewing things, ways of thinking and state of being. The former is adaptive to the Three-Layer Structure of Enterprise Competitiveness while the latter is inappropriate to it. The adaptivity of a firm's culture is to the Three-Layer Structure of Enterprise Competitiveness, the more its performance becomes enhanced in the long term. Yet, it is the constituents of a firm that form and back up its competitiveness structure. Its personnel's modes of viewing, ways of thinking and state of being are collectively reflected in the competitiveness structure of the firm. There is a linkage here between corporate culture and competitiveness.

Corporate culture changes. It changes if there occurs some transformation in the constituents' modes of viewing, ways of thinking and state of being. If it is a healthy transformation, it is to be encouraged. If not, it is to be stopped and turned around the right way. Healthiness of a firm's culture is measured by the degree of its adaptability to the Three-Layer Structure of Enterprise Competitiveness. Accordingly, business leaders would be recommended to keep in mind the most significant attributes of corporate culture which are adaptive to the Competitiveness Structure.

In Chapter 9 and 11, we took up Ohmi Merchants, Hewlett-Packard, Xerox, Nissan and the Confucianist Company, and accounted for the attributes of their corporate culture respectively.

Now, here, we shall explain in full detail the representative attributes of healthy corporate culture.

12.1 Attributes of healthy corporate culture

Future-Orientedness and Youngness, Yomigaeri

To live long, a firm needs to take a fresh life before its days expire. To take in a fresh life is a deed of Future-Orientedness in the US culture and that of Yomigaeri in the Japanese culture.

In starting out with a new venture, entrepreneurs earnestly believe in innovation, self-reformation and independence. When their firm has developed, gone through a growth stage and reached a stage of stability, however, the situation will be different. Ideas and ways of business in their organization may turn out to differ from those in the early days of the firm and probably not be flexible enough to cope with a new market and a changing environment. The old rules and methods are firmly imbedded in it. Many cases are cited where such a firm did not break from the conventional ways, and, as a result, fell into obscurity, which attests to its inability to take in a fresh life. Among top managers, in that context, whether of a rising firm or of an established one, there are those who are so self-righteous as to think that things would not go well without them. That way of thinking, in turn, would prevent the firm from regenerating itself.

There are generally two main reasons for the failure of a firm. One is that a top manager is focused exclusively on an immediate profit and does not attempt to transform the organization. The other is that he or she recklessly diversifies into too many lines of business only to shorten or complete the span of the organization life. In both cases, the top manager's thoughts on business are not refreshed nor meta-morphosed to meet the reality of the organization. In other words, he does not introduce a fresh life into his ways of viewing and thinking. It is an arduous task, indeed, for top managers to have a wide outlook, take a risk and develop the way for the future of the firm. With oppositions and hurdles set before them, most of them are likely to patch things up for the moment or take a temporary remedy. In an extreme case, they would think and appeal to a cartel, a competition-restrictive law and a government relief measure of the weak firms, and so forth. Those protective and irrational measures, however, would eventually confine the firm to a suffocative and binding environment. With its development extremely limited, the firm will dwindle away, in the final analysis, into a minimal existence or nothing.

How to cut off such a protective and irrational way of thinking, and how to revitalize its organization is a matter of Future-Orientedness and that of Yomigaeri. It is the deed of Future-Orientedness or of

Yomigaeri that can help lengthen the life of a firm. It is the only and the best way in regenerating an organization. An industrial structure changes. A market changes. Firms have no choice but to cope with the change of the times.

Newness, Musubi

Work means to look for and do something new or things that others have not yet done. In so doing, one ought to, at first, clear the way of customary practices. The meaning of Newness or Musubi is rightfully understood in that perspective. It is with the mind of Newness or that of Musubi that one can overcome things of customary practice and create new ones.

Now, let us elaborate on this matter further. A firm needs to observe its main line of products as objectively as practicable, recognize what stage of the life cycle they are now in, and develop and nurture a new generation of products accordingly. In the early stages of a product's life cycle, the main concern is how to improve its effectiveness. In the later stages, however, the firm has to switch its weight from pursuing effectiveness among the conventional products to creating a new line of products. It is to be noted, however, that an organization suited to pursuing the effectiveness of an existing line of products tends not to give a due consideration to innovation or creation of new things different in nature.

To overcome such a tendency and change the course of business, there must be something in the organization that the top manager can fully trust. He may have faith in a certain technology or technical knowledge base or a talented group of people in the firm. What technology and how capable talent an organization has is an essential condition for the top manager to decide what line of products to develop and what market to enter for the future of the firm. A main line of products for next and future generations can not be created only by a borrowed technology. If a firm would embark in a new business with a borrowed technology and fail, there would be nothing left in the organization. If it has a first-rate technology of its own which is evaluated as such the world over, things would be altogether different. Even if it should fail in trying to generate something new with that technology, the firm will have accumulated the technical knowledge on it and its people involved will be more talented, whether technically or otherwise, than before. The accumulated technical knowledge and talent are necessary ingredients for the success of future business.

To try to create things new over and again is the way of Newness and the mind of Musubi, while it certainly contributes to the accumulation of necessary ingredients, i.e., technology and talent, for the success of a business.

As to human talent, in that context, education and training of personnel have been emphasized these days as J. Naisbitt and P. Aburdene refer to in their book, *Re-inventing the Corporation.*

> Companies with the most nurturing environments for personal growth become known as great places to work ... like the companies in The Best 100 Companies to Work for in America. At companies like People Express, Hewitt Associates, Hewlett-Packard, 3M, and W.L.Gore & Associates, the corporate commitment to personal growth is reflected in a dynamic environment for work and learning.
>
> • The credo at People Express is that 'work must create a learning opportunity for the individuals involved. While certain aspects may be routine, the total work package must be varied enough to provide mental stimulus for personal growth.'
>
> • 'You are your own manager. Rarely does anyone need monitoring ... If a mistake is made, it's everyone's mistake,' says Linda Menees, a secretary at Hewitt Associates, the employee benefits consultant. Ms. Menees says she has always been treated the same as any of the company's partners.
>
> • Hewlett-Packard has created such a positive environment for personal growth that a recent survey of some 8,000 HP workers about company practices placed HP in the top one-half of 1 percent of more than 1,000 US companies.
>
> • The strong point at Minnesota Mining & Manufacturing Company is its ability to nurture creativity, says Forbes magazine. 3M seems to have mastered the dictum 'Grow or die.' 3M's philosophy, as expressed by CEO Lew Lehr, is 'Our concern for independent thinking and the entrepreneurial spirit is not just one approach among many. It is our only approach.'
>
> • W.L.Gore & Associates fosters personal growth by structuring people's tasks around commitment, not authority. Sometimes when new people join the company, they are told to 'look around and find something interesting to do.'(Of course, other times people are hired for specific tasks.) People grow when their work interests them and they are committed, rather than assigned, to it.   (Ibid. PP 54-55)

Jay Forrester at MIT stated that education and training were at the center of corporate strategy. He even said that about 25 percent of the total working time of all members in the firm ought to be spent for their preparation of future work. (Ibid.)

Integrity and Fairness, Akaki-Kokoro

It is said that a firm can not grow beyond its top man's capacity and character. The top manager assumes the leading part in nurturing and supporting the corporate culture of his organization. The corporate culture is thus influenced by his character to a considerable extent. It matters to that degree, therefore, if he is a man of Integrity and Fairness, or a man of Akaki-Kokoro.

A company is a social being. To live generation after generation, it needs to be fair and clean in its conduct. A company's profit-making is to be done in a fair way. When the company's logic of profit-making is associated, in some way, with Fairness and Cleanness in the top manager's mind, the firm could be said to have an attribute of social nature in a real sense. Akaki-Kokoro and Value of Cleanness are thus the core of a firm's social nature.

Within the organization of a firm, fair treatment of personnel is a foundation of fairness. It activates communication among the personnel and makes the organization open and clean. It is good and legitimate to judge personnel's abilities and promisingness in a just and fair way with no regard to age and career. It is not good nor proper, in that context, for people to exchange gifts with each other. When one's senior or colleague is promoted, one had better not congratulate him excessively.

It is a vital principle that personnel are to be evaluated on their performance. Accordingly, the company ought to develop and prepare as many arenas as possible where the personnel can be actively engaged.

In meeting customers, the personnel are expected to correspond to them with sincerity. If they receive a claim on products or services from their customer, they should cope with it in earnest and try to come up with a solution of which the customer is duly convinced. Customers' claims can be a good medium for the firm to improve its technical capacity and develop excellent products or services.

A man truly liked in his country is liked by people the world over. What is expected on the international arena, in fact, is that business people have Integrity and Fairness, or Akaki-Kokoro, with which they can truly communicate with each other.

Both Individualism and Yaoyorozu-No-Kami highly regard an individual's personality and creativity. For an individual to build a fine personality and develop creative abilities, in turn, there are two matters to be considered. One is the matter of self-knowledge, and the other is that of a place suitable for exercising creativity.

The individual, to begin with, ought to state his views and opinions with a sincere mind. In a business environment, in particular, if one copies ideas from others and does not think on his or her own, one's personality would not reveal itself. When one expresses a thought and its process, others would take it as one's opinion and understand and recognize it as such. In other words, if a person knows himself or herself sufficient to form independent views or beliefs, the person would be well understood by others while performing and enjoying a good life. With their own views or beliefs in doing their work, people could enjoy working.

The organization is, in that respect, to be a place for people to express their views and opinions freely and frankly. If not, no ideas or proposals could possibly be expected to come out which would be decidedly needed to meet today's ever-changing market. A place must be prepared, to put it further, for one to exert his creativity to the fullest extent. How can we prepare it, then ?

The first approach is to form a flat organization. It is by drastically reducing management posts on the managerial ladder that the organization can be turned into its flattest form. One way is to relinquish the hierarchy in the board of directors and establish a flat board consisting of directors with no titles. As a result, there would be no senior executive director, no executive director, no managing director and so on. The same can be executed among management ranks. With the organization being flat, it could be much easier to transfer managers from one post to another, which, in turn, is conducive to the most appropriate post change. It also helps facilitate free discussion and equality among people.

We can cite W.L.Gore & Associates, Inc. as an example of the companies having formed such a flat organization.

> Delaware-based W.L.Gore & Associates, Inc., the maker of Gore-tex fabric, the sports and military material that keeps out rain but allows the body to breathe, is a well-publicized example of the new corporation. The company has no titles, no bosses, no map of managerial authority, and two objectives ; to make money and to have fun. W.L.Gore's secret

is that people manage themselves by organizing around voluntary commitments. Some new hires are told to go find something interesting to do. 'Commitment, not authority, produces results,' says company founder Bill Gore. W.L.Gore & Associates achieves its money-making goal : Sales in the last ten years have grown 35 percent annually. (J. Naisbitt and P. Aburdene, 1986   PP 11-12)

The organization of W.L.Gore & Associates, Inc. is named the 'lattice organization' as explained below.

This is the new organizational model developed by W.L.Gore & Associates, which has successfully used small-team management since it opened its doors in 1958. Employees are called 'associates,' and everyone in the company deals with everyone else directly through a cross-hatching of horizontal and vertical lines...hence founder Bill Gore's name for the company's management structure, 'lattice organization.' We had read with great interest about W.L.Gore & Associates in *Inc. magazine* and in *The Tarrytown Letter*, a publication of Bob Schwart'z group in Tarrytown, New York. But we felt we would never really understand this lattice idea without visiting W.L.Gore & Associates. After all, what does it really mean to say that people deal directly with everyone else ? In Newark, Delaware, we met Bill Gore and Vieve Gore, Bill's wife of fifty years and business partner for more than twenty-five years. In their early seventies, but much younger in their thinking, appearance, and energy level, they told us how the lattice structure works in transforming Bill's vision of work in a small task force into a companywide esprit de corps. 'Every (successful) organization has a lattice organization that underlies the facade of authoritarian hierarchy,' says Bill Gore. 'It is through these lattice organizations that things get done and most of us delight in going around the formal procedures and doing things the straightforward and easy way.(Ibid. P 43)

What W.L.Gore has done, it seems, is legitimize the essential...the informal structure...found in most organizations and eliminated the superfluous...the hierarchy. In Gore's lattice, people communicate person-to-person. No one holds any formal position of authority. Leadership emerges naturally when people attract followers. But what really holds the lattice together is Gore's emphasis on commitment and its sponsor system. All work assignments are voluntary, so tasks and functions are organized by commitments. At W.L.Gore & Associates, you make your own commitments and keep them, and you do not make commitments you cannot keep. Similarly, an important lattice precept is :

'Objectives are set by those who must make them happen.' Gore's sponsor system is the second key element of the lattice. When a new person joins the company (which as it turns out is often because of the firm's extraordinary growth rate : 30 percent of Gore's 4,000 employees were new in 1984), an experienced associate volunteers to take responsibility for this new person learning his or her job. It is your sponsor, not a person in authority over you, who decides whether, after a three-month learning period, your contribution to the company equals your salary. If it does not, it is probably harder on the sponsor, whose responsibility it was to teach, than on the learner. There are three different types of sponsors at Gore. The Starting Sponsor described above ; the Advocate Sponsor, whose job it is to know about and appreciate a person's accomplishments and contributions in the organization and speak for them ; the Compensation Sponsor, who knows all the associates working on a team and consults with the Advocate Sponsor and, with other members of a compensation team, lists people's accomplishments and determines a commensurate salary. (Ibid. PP 44-45)

It is especially not about being nice to people who do not produce. At W.L.Gore, an associate's salary matches his or her contribution to the company. When after a three-month probationary period new associates fail to learn their jobs, they are not fired, but their salaries are reduced to equal their contributions to the company...zero. 'Usually, they will leave then,' says Bill Gore. (Ibid. P 45)

Taken together, Bill Gore says,

The simplicity and order of an authoritarian organization make it an almost irresistible temptation. Yet it is counter to the principles of individual freedom and smothers the creative growth of man. (Ibid. P 35)

W.L.Gore & Associates is certainly one of the good cases having materialized a new flat organization, but the trend to flat organizations of various types has been, indeed, a large current in recent years.

We are witnessing the beginnings of a tremendous whittling away of middle management, a flattening out of those hierarchies that were the norm in industrial America. Worldwide, middle management has shrunk more than 15 percent since 1979. And there is much more to come. Middle managers...the people who collect, process, and pass information up and down the hierarchy...are losing out to smart technology in the race for productivity. Middle managers have benefited from the belief that people work better when they are closely supervised. But now those hierarchies which middle managers held in place are breaking into a wide array of largely self-managing structures...networks, multidisciplinary teams, and small groups. The whittling away of middle management is accomplished in a variety of ways : early retirement, hiring freezes, outplacement. But it is all to the same end :

- Weyerhaeuser has let go 1,500 workers in the past three years. Half of them were middle managers.
- Western Airlines let go 13 VPs and 500 middle managers in December 1981 when it was in serious financial straits.
- Ford Motor Company has decreased the number of middle managers since 1978. They are seeking to expand the average supervisory control of the manager from three to five people, thinning out middle management.
- Brunswick Corp. cut its headquarters staff by 40 percent and division heads report directly to the CEO.
- TRW, Inc., is continuing its long-term strategy toward 'simplifying our organization.'

Much of this was done in the name of recession or tough times. But tough times sometimes give management an excuse to do what should be done anyway. And new companies just starting out are building very flat pyramids where people, in effect, manage themselves. (Ibid. PP 15-16)

The above tendency has been apparently facilitated by the development and application of computers.

Once indispensable to senior executives, many middle managers are now watching computers do their job in a fraction of the time and at a percentage of the cost. The whittling away of middle management presents serious problems for all those baby boomers about to enter middle management. The number of men and women between thirty-five and forty-six, the prime age range for entering middle management, will increase 42 percent between 1985 and 1995. Clearly, millions of baby boomers who aimed for middle management will never reach their goal. There simply will not be enough middle management jobs. It is a scary thought for some people. Corporations would suffer, too, losing talent and failing to reap the sizable investment already made in these valuable human resources ... unless they can invent alternative ways to use people productively. One way is to put talented people together in small groups ... which are entering their own boom years. Others could work as entrepreneurs within a company. The whittling away of middle

126

management is further reinforcing the trend for companies to smash the hierarchical pyramids and adopt new people structures such as networks, intrapreneurs, and small teams. (Ibid. PP 17-18)

That is,

It is as if all of the boxes in the organization chart were thrown into the air and programmed to fall into a new set of patterns that best facilitate communication ... networks, hubs, lattices, circles, and wheels. Computers and the whittling away of middle management are toppling hierarchies, flattening the pyramid. At Apple Computer, for example, fifteen people report to CEO John Sculley. When the best corporate talent has no corporate hierarchy to climb, what happens to their competitive energy ? One answer is to transform it into a creative, enterprising spirit and channel it into small work groups where communication is quicker and more effective, and where the increasing number of baby boomers are experiencing the 'small is beautiful' entrepreneurial environment that is consistent with their values...and highly productive for the company. Networking is the baby boom's management style of choice. The millions of baby boomers who do make it into the smaller ranks of middle management and beyond...as well as the millions who have created and will create their own companies...will be in a position to influence the structures and management styles the rest of the corporate world will live within. Their choice is networks, small teams, and other decentralized structures. (Ibid. PP 36-37)

Corresponding to the changes mentioned above, companies such as CRS Sirrine, Advanced Micro Devices, and the others have explored in their own way a range of structures including cross-disciplinary teams, partnerships, and fellowship options which would promote better communication, innovation, and increased productivity. Small teams have been, in fact, attempted and utilized to a considerable degree.

Flexible, fast, loaded with talent, the small-team model is the most popular and widespread alternative to bureaucratic organization. From the auto factories of Detroit to the software firms in Silicon Valley, corporations are successfully reorganizing the flow of power and communication within companies through this flexible new structure. One simple reason for their success is that people like working in small teams. Advanced Micro Devices, the Silicon Valley-based silicon chip maker, has only 5,000 employees, but there are more than twenty company teams, from the Mail and Literature Distribution Team to the

127

MOS Static RAM Design Team. Teams belong to 'directorates' with their own engineering, manufacturing, and sales component and are led by a managing director who works directly with Jerry Saunders, the company's founder and head. (Ibid. P 38)

Now, the second approach, to prepare a place for one to exert his or her creativity, is to split off part of an organization to form a new one. When an organization has grown too big for people to do their work actively and effectively, it could be a good choice to cut off part of it and build a new firm. In such a newly built firm, entrepreneurial spirit would be expected to be in force. It also helps regenerate the ethos prevailed in the early days of the original firm. To split part of an organization and form a new firm is a form of metabolism which is applicable to every kind of organization.

We shall take up, here, some cases of the firms splitting off their organization and forming new ones. (R. J. Laubacher, T. W. Malone and the MIT Scenario Working Group, 1997)

The film industry

The film industry may stand as an early adopter of new organizational forms. During the studio era of the 1920s through 1940s, for example, the industry was organized much like the vertically-integrated, mass production enterprises established in the manufacturing sector during the late nineteenth and early twentieth century. With the decline of the studios in the 1950s, however, came the arrival of a new system, in which the large entertainment conglomerates' role was reduced to finance and distribution, and responsibility for production shifted to a number of small firms organized on an ad hoc basis. On large projects in the film industry today, hundreds or even thousands of individuals and small entities each contribute their part to the completion of a multi-million dollar production. During the post-studio period, the power of the talent agencies, which played an important role as deal brokers, increased significantly. With the recent growth in the number and importance of films produced independently with private capital, and the fragmentation of the distribution system to accommodate this new type of picture, the industry may be entering yet another new stage.

Textile production in the Prato region of Italy

Another example is the Menichetti textile enterprise in the Prato region of Italy. In the early 1970s, Massimo Menichetti inherited his family's business, a failing textile mill. Menichetti quickly broke up the firm into eight separate companies. He sold a significant portion of equity ... between one third to one half ... to key employees and required that at least 50 percent of the new companies' sales come from customers outside the old firm. Within three years, the eight new businesses had accomplished a complete turnaround, achieving significant increases in machine utilization and productivity. The Menichetti pattern was replicated at numerous other integrated mills in Prato, and by 1990, over 15,000 small textile firms, each with an average of fewer than 5 employees, were active in the region. This constituted a threefold increase in activity from the previous decade, during a time when the textile industry was in decline throughout the rest of Europe. The Prato firms have built state-of-the-art factories and warehouses, and developed cooperative ventures in realms such as purchasing, logistics, and R&D, where scale economies could be exploited. Textiles from the region have become the preferred material for renowned fashion designers around the world. Key actors in the Prato scheme are brokers, known as impannatori, who act as conduit between customers and the small manufacturing concerns. They effectively direct the design and manufacturing process by bringing together the appropriate groups of firms to meet customers' specific needs. By the late 1980s, the impannatori had even created an electronic market, which gathered data on projected factory utilization and upcoming requirements, and allowed textile production capacity to be traded like a commodity.

Semco

Another firm which has followed a course of radical decentralization is Semco, a Brazilian manufacturer of marine and food-service equipment. By the late 1980s, Semco was already an innovative firm, run on the principles of employee participation, profit sharing, and open information systems. But Semco was forced to try even more radical innovations in 1990, when the Brazilian finance ministry instituted severe austerity measures and effectively reduced the nation's money supply by 80 percent overnight. To survive the resulting crisis, management developed the idea of encouraging employees to form satellite enterprises which used company facilities, with Semco providing an initial contract to get the new ventures going and offering severance packages and training to assist employees in making the transition. The scheme allowed the parent company to cut payroll and inventory costs, and at the same time work with suppliers who knew Semco's business intimately. The entrepreneurial energy unleashed in the satellite firms has been a major additional advantage for Semco. In 1990, the parent firm had 500 employees ; four years later it had 200, with the satellites employing the same number and 50-60 more working part time for both Semco and one of the satellites. But by 1994, the satellites were accounting for two-thirds of the new products Semco launched. The experiment created a more free-wheeling, experimental culture within the entire organization, the result being that the majority owner of the firm, Ricardo Semler writes with pride that 'no one in the company really knows how many people we employ.' The lack of direction from management and the ad hoc, seemingly chaotic environment, has enhanced morale and performance in both the core company and the satellites.

In that context, the intrapreneurial idea has been adopted to a great extent among companies, in particular, in the airline business in recent years.

Intrapreneurs are people with entrepreneurial skills employed in corporations. But instead of leaving the company to undertake their ventures, they create these new businesses within the company. It is win/win arrangement. The company retains a talented employee and an innovative new business ; the employee gets the satisfaction of developing his or her idea without having to risk leaving the company and going into business. (J. Naisbitt and J. Aburdene, 1986   P 74)

The whole principle behind intrapreneurship is to use a company's existing resources...human, financial, and physical...to launch new businesses and generate new income. So it is logical that mature industries facing a more competitive market such as airlines are ideal candidates for intrapreneurial innovation. 'This industry needs every cent it can generate. We've got to be creative about using our huge asset base to develop new revenues,' says American Airlines president Robert Crandall. That remark shows that Crandall is asking the right question... 'What business are we really in ?' Whatever the problems in the airline business, that is a good sign. But what do airlines do that could grow into an intrapreneurial venture ? They maintain their aircraft, train flight crews, and mastermind enormously complex telephone reservation services...all of which have become intrapreneurial subdivisions of major airlines :

- United Airlines makes $ 15 million per year training flight crews for other airlines.
- American's training arm, American Airlines Training Corp., made

$ 1.8 million in profits on $ 37.7 million worth of training sales in 1983.

- American, United, TWA, Delta, and Eastern lease computerized reservation systems to travel agents. The system generated $ 100 million of income in 1983 at American Airlines alone.

- American's phone system, American Airlines Telemarketing Services, has signed up a natural though unusual client...the system will be used to take pledges for a religious fund-raising telethon.

- Frontier Airlines leases its planes through Frontier Leasco, Inc., while US Air took in $ 25.5 million in 1983 as an aircraft broker selling twenty-one planes.

- Contract maintenance is becoming a growth area because of deregulation : American Airlines expects to gross $ 100 million in ground services by 1986. Admittedly, airlines have been operating some of these inside businesses for some time. And, so far as we know, they are not doing anything special to nurture the inside entrepreneurs their industry needs. Nevertheless, businesses are accomplishing what intrapreneurs set out to do ; use the company's existing resources to generate new products and services...and ultimately more income.

Airlines that creatively combine existing assets with the spark of new ideas will survive and flourish, while those which continually wail about the perils of deregulation...the loss of protected markets...will go out of business. (Ibid. PP 75-76)

In addition to the airline industry's case above, we can further cite an intrapreneurial idea applied in small businesses.

Terra Tek is a small Salt Lake City-based high technology firm engaged in research services, product development, and new energy ventures. It employs only 150 people but that does not stop Terra Tek from awarding its own 'innovation grants' modeled after the National Science Foundation's Small Business Innovation Awards Program. The two to five innovation grants of not more than $ 10,000 each are awarded annually. They enable employees to pursue their own projects while innovating and enhancing the company's research capabilities. When a project becomes commercially viable, the employee assumes control of the new venture, which in time may even become a separate company owned jointly by the innovator and the parent company ; the equity, however, remains in the hands of the innovator. (Ibid. PP 76-77)

The third factor, in preparing an appropriate arena for personnel's creativity, is their voluntary activities. If a project team, not shown on the organization chart, is actively engaged in its objective, it will be indicative of the utter healthiness of the firm. The business environment changes all the time. If, under such an environment, a company wishes to take a chance in other areas than its own, the conventional structure of its organization will not be well suited. To compensate that non-suitability, it surely needs voluntary activities among people, i.e., Yaoyorozu-No-Kami. In fact, it is often said that the secret of success in a new product development is found in the engineers' voluntary circle activities. Everyone ought to be encouraged, therefore, to participate in such a circle, whether it is of his professional area or otherwise. Participants are to be permitted, preferably, to do their activities during working hours as well as after work. Personnel management is, in the final analysis, to provide workers a place where they can enjoy working.

In this connection, circle activities have been tried out in some innovative companies in the US.

While many American companies grafted the Japan-developed quality control circle into their corporate culture (some 10,000 people from 4,000 companies belong to the Cincinnati-based International Association of Quality Circles), others called it a fad and rejected it out of hand. But America had heard the message : The people who know the most about any job are the people doing it. To keep a business healthy, you have to get at that information and apply it throughout the company. And the best way to do that might not be with quality control circles, so many innovative companies began to experiment with other ways to exchange information and custom-fitted these new forms to their company's needs.

- At Olga, the maker of women's undergarments, it is called a Creative Meeting, and it was originally the way designers brainstormed new fashion ideas. But Jan Erteszek, the company's cofounder (with his wife, the real Olga behind each Olga fashion), decided to try Creative Meetings company-wide and ask people how they would run the company if they had his job. Now small groups of associates (they are not called employees at Olga) meet once a week for six weeks, usually two to three times each year.

- At the Portland-based Electro Scientific Industries, each spring groups of twelve to fifteen employees tell the company's president what is working and what is not, in their 'Going Well/In the Way' meetings (as in 'What's going well ? What's in the way ?').

- Drivers at Preston Trucking Co. meet in groups of twenty every few weeks to discuss how to do their jobs better.
- Kollmorgen Corp. calls them People Meetings...the monthly get-togethers to discuss what is happening in the company. (Ibid. PP 46-47)

Taking Things Easy, Kotodama and Matsuri

In a good company, there is such an atmosphere that people feel free to make a fair and straight argument, and are prepared to come to grips with whatever matters with no hesitance. Under those circumstances, people would say, 'Enjoy your job', in a real sense, which is an expression of Taking Things Easy, an attribute of the US culture or that of Kotodama and Matsuri, the corresponding attributes of Japanese culture.

In such a firm, also, a manager would say, 'Let's sit down for a moment and have a talk', and he would get his staff to take a seat. Both of them, thus, would feel at ease and can afford to talk about whatever things they like. Since they would talk at eye level with each other, their communication can be properly exchanged. Their feeling at ease helps facilitate communication between them. When a manager sits down and a staff stands while talking primarily due to their being conscious of status and rank, it makes for the manager's psychological advantage while the staff is disadvantaged. It may cause inequality and, at times, invite misunderstanding between them.

In a similar manner, a flat organization can help promote communication between managers and staff. They, in fact, could have a talk on an equal footing. There is a story of a mill manager, in that context, who makes it a practice go around the mill for about an hour after the close of his work. He inspects the facilities and equipment and talks to people on the shop floor. He listens to those people and at times drinks beer with them. That easiness surely facilitates communication and helps things to be done smoothly.

No taboo

There is no taboo in the US as testified in the fact that the country has accepted immigrants in an unbroken succession from all over the world since its foundation. There is no taboo also in the Japanese culture as shown in the way of thinking of Kanjyo that one is to absorb whatever things good and useful with no exception. The state of being of no taboo is real and genuine in both countries.

In the business field, however, when a firm grows old, authoritarianism and bureaucracy tend to prevail in the organization. In the stability or declining stage of a firm, in fact, one can see many rules of prohibition and taboo within the organization. With those prohibitions and taboos, the conservative power would try to keep stability and maintain the status quo. The number of taboos, in that context, is an indicator of the degree of a firm's unhealthiness. The attitude of sticking to stability and the status quo is squarely opposed to competition. When a firm has aged, therefore, it is particularly significant to bring competitive principles into the organization. The competitive principles could be an effective tool to rid an aged and unhealthy company of taboos.

In terms of cultural attributes, it is Individualism, Future-Orientedness, Youngness and Newness among the US culture that collectively promote competition. It is likewise Yaoyorozu-No-Kami, Yomigaeri and Musubi in the Japanese culture that facilitate it. To live through generations, a firm ought to cast off taboos incessantly.

In order to break down taboo, in that context, the following bureaucracy smashers would be of assistance and use. (J. Naisbitt and P. Aburdene, 1986)

1   Set up a system of reverse reviews. Everyone who is evaluated gets to evaluate the boss, too.
2   Call everyone by first name.
3   Try out the rule : Use little paper, keep no files.
4   Call people associates, partners, managers, or just plain people instead of employees or workers.
5   Decentralize authority absolutely.
6   Eliminate executive dining rooms, executive rest rooms, special parking spots and the like.
7   Insist everybody to answer his or her own phone.
8   Get people to manage themselves : to set and monitor their own goals, to manage their work load and set their own priorities.
9   Adopt the policy : Only do business with people who are pleasant.
10   Take a deep breath and throw out the old organization chart.

A good company is the one with healthy corporate culture, and a bad company is the one with unhealthy corporate culture. Yet, the corporate culture changes. One should attentively monitor, therefore, if its corporate culture is in a fully healthy state.

The representative attributes explained thus far would certainly help in so doing.

13 Oticon, a 21st century-type company

Many years have past since the business process redesign or reengineering was widely propagated as a means to enhance corporate performance. Few firms that employed it, however, have succeeded in improving their performance. Why is that ?

In investigating the causes of failure of BPR (business process redesign), it is found out that the concept of business process redesign is inappropriate to the Three-Layer Structure of Enterprise Competitiveness in the following three points.

The first is that BPR is based on the principles of 'scientific management'. As N. Bjorn-Andersen and J. A. Turner pointed out, BPR neglects the human side of an organization.

> That is, it does not consider such factors as culture, power, politics, social structure, and motivation. While scientific management may result in an efficiently designed task, little consideration is given to the individuals who perform the task, how they work with others, and the factors that influence their behavior. (N. Bjorn-Andersen and J. A. Turner, 1995 P 5)

It seems that BPR is only concerned with the narrowly defined technical aspect of an organization.

The second is that BPR is a top-down and expert-led approach. Changes in the process, indeed, need to be started at the bottom of an organization. Small groups respectively focused on a specific line of work are the leading actors in expediting those changes. Without their genuine support, any process redesign could not have been successfully achieved. There is no such a way of thought in BPR.

The third is that the reengineering defines its desired goal in advance and takes changes as a static process. The successful change of an organization, on the contrary, is not a static process but a dynamic process.

It makes little sense, as prescribed by BPR, to specify end configuration in advance. Ends need to emerge as the result of the change process itself. It may well be that the process, rather than the end configuration, is the stable portion of change. (Ibid. P 5)

What is needed in raising performance is recognized in the process itself. In reality, an organization develops on and on, with no end, which is its only state of being.

To deliberate further on the points above, we shall examine the study of Oticon, a Danish company, by Niels Bjorn-Andersen and Jon A. Turner. In the study, they argue that it is 'Metamorphosis' that helps enhance corporate performance, while duly pointing out the defects ascribed to the thought of BPR. (N. Bjorn-Andersen and J. A. Turner, 1995) The Metamorphosis means, in our words, to phenomenally raise an organization's adaptability to the Three-Layer Structure of Enterprise Competitiveness. Through Metamorphosis, i.e., a frame-breaking, Oticon made a complete breakaway from its conventional practices.

So, in taking up the study of Oticon, let us first see how the firm has transformed itself into an organization appropriate to the Three-Layer Structure of Enterprise Competitiveness, i.e., how the Metamorphosis has been executed. And, then, we shall refer to the difference between Metamorphosis and BPR, and finally explain corporate culture found in that Metamorphosis.

Oticon is one of the five world-largest manufacturers of hearing aids. With headquarters in Denmark, it has about 1200 employees and annual sales of approximately DKK 480 million which is about $ 80 million. Out of the total sales, more than 90 percent is from export through subsidiaries and agents, covering over 100 countries. There are production facilities and a basic research department of its own at Oticon. They had placed emphasis on the quality of their products, relying on their engineering and product design until the late 1980s. In fact, Oticon was No.1 in the industry in 1979, and a market leader ever since.

However, towards the end of the 80s customer demand changed from wanting a relatively large, high quality device behind the ear to a more discrete unit inside the ear. This trend was strongly exploited by a US competitor. (Ibid.)

As a result, Oticon's market share decreased abruptly and suffered its first financial loss in 1986. Against this background, Lars Kolind was recruited and appointed as a new CEO in 1988. He instituted cost controls in a drastic manner and managed to turn the firm into the black in 1989.

Two to three years after that, however, Kolind realized that cost-cutting measures had been fully exploited. He decided, then, to initiate a total reform of Oticon. He thought that the real issue was to transform the company from a manufacturing concern producing high-quality standard hearing aids to a first-rate service firm with products.

> The organization Kolind envisioned, one in which the various functional units worked together in a truly integrated manner to craft innovative customer driven products and one that was more responsive to customer demands, could not be achieved by normal structural or procedural change. It was necessary to create a completely new, innovative, flexible, and learning organization. (Ibid. P 6)

Kolind explained :

> It would be a company where jobs were shaped to fit the person instead of the other way around. Each person would be given more functions, and a job would emerge by the individual accumulating a portfolio of functions. (Ibid. P 6)

Kolind named that a 'spaghetti organization' since the multiple roles to be carried out by people are highly interwined.

To create a flexible and innovative organization, accordingly, four types of organizational changes were instituted at Oticon as the following.

Organizational change 1 : Elimination of the traditional departments

At first, the traditional departments were eliminated, and the head office was turned into a single large department. All of the works were, thus, organized as projects, by which a form of flat organization was realized. (Three-Layer Structure of Enterprise Competitiveness III-B)

The project organization would not pursue narrowly defined interests as the traditional organization consisting of departments did, but contribute to the interests of the company as a whole. A project team is, due to its temporary nature, flexible enough to respond to unexpected demands.

Marketing, for example, is an area where work load fluctuates throughout the year. August through November are particularly busy with preparations for exhibitions and trade shows. During the autumn, marketing could easily use 30 people. Now, instead of having a large fixed number of employees working in marketing throughout the year, a much smaller staff permanently work there, around 5, including the project head. As the workload increases over summer and autumn, more people are recruited internally from the other project groups, e.g., from R&D, to staff an expanded and concentrated marketing effort. (Ibid. P 7)

The maximum utilization of people's time is thought out here. (Three-Layer Structure of Enterprise Competitiveness III-A)

Organizational change 2 : Organization of work in form of projects

A project team consists of a project leader, who is appointed by the top management, and a group of workers. It is the project leader who is in charge of collecting people necessary to carry out his project. Using his workstation, the project leader publicizes the project on an electronic bulletin board while workers, who would like to join the project, sign on it with their workstations. When leaving the project, it is a rule for the worker either to get consent from the project leader or to find out another to replace him.

In the project organization, anyone could be a project leader if he or she finds a new business opportunity which the top management agree to support. (Three-Layer Structure of Enterprise Competitiveness I. Enhancement of initiative)

Since this makes it possible to quickly allocate resources among projects as deemed necessary, the new organization greatly improves Oticon's response to unanticipated requirements from customers. (Three-Layer Structure of Enterprise Competitiveness III-B)

Organizational change 3 : Employees occupy several positions

Employees have 4 to 5 tasks simultaneously. In other words, they are engaged in 4 to 5 projects of diverse nature so that they are often required to exercise different skills, respectively, on each of them. Here is a versatile way of organizing works to make better use of employees' set of skills. (Three-Layer Structure of Enterprise Competitiveness III-B)

Kolind says, 'There is no room for employees that stick to the old concept of one job, one person.' (Ibid. P 7) Staff in accounting and production could participate in preparing marketing and promotion materials. Hearing aids are a commodity destined for consumers. Many different modes of viewing would help in that respect. A person in accounting might have a way of viewing unexpected by marketing. People of different backgrounds can exchange views among them, which is conducive to the spread of new ideas, reform, intelligence and others in the organization. (Three-Layer Structure of Enterprise Competitiveness II. Diffusion of new ideas, planning and others)

Organizational change 4 : New control philosophy

Workers have a choice to decide what projects they will join. They are not assigned any project from above. Given that choice, they would be more interested in their work than otherwise. It would appeal to their willingness to work. (Three-Layer Structure of Enterprise Competitiveness I. Enhancement of initiative)

In such an ethos, personnel's responsibility and motivation would be high in doing their tasks. (Three-Layer Structure of Enterprise Competitiveness III-C)

On the other hand, there is no longer a need for project leaders to act a part of supervisor. Workers do their tasks on their own. Managerial resources are, thus, freed, which could be directed toward more creative works. (Three-Layer Structure of Enterprise Competitiveness I. Enterprise ethos) The project leaders are now expected to act as an innovator or as a motivator.

Along with the dramatic four types of organizational changes explained above, in that context, two distinctive change strategies were adopted at Oticon. One is a new open plan office layout, and the other is an elimination of 95 percent of all paper.

No private desks

The firm decided to get rid of private offices including that of Kolind in the head office. All the walls were removed to create a single large open space. Every employee now has a small lockable caddie with one drawer for personal things and a couple of shelves for storing up ten files. Whenever he addresses a project work, he wheels the caddie to an empty desk in the vicinity of the other members. No one is in a fixed location. They change physical location according to the projects. All the desks are similar and installed with a workstation through which access to worker specific information can be obtained. (Three-Layer Structure of Enterprise Competitiveness III-A)

The principle is that if employees need to work together on a number of projects with different people, it was not practical to have everyone in a fixed location. (Ibid. P 8)

Elimination of paper

Whenever they are seated, employees can get access to their file through the workstation. They can receive and scan all the documents whenever they like and they have access authority.

Once the ID code has been entered, access is provided to central files and a personal calendar along with tools for creating, transmitting, duplicating, and storing documents that may contain text, drawings, and graphics. (Ibid. P 8)

Thus, the workers are discouraged from keeping paper files. As a result, the elimination of 95 percent of paper was materialized throughout the office. (Three-Layer Structure of Enterprise Competitiveness III-A)

As has been described, the Metamorphosis at Oticon has decidedly heightened its adaptiveness to the Three-Layer Structure of Enterprise Competitiveness. It is such a scale of innovation as to be called frame-breaking. In 1992 when that frame-breaking was instituted, the company's profits were nine times as much as in 1989 and 1990 with sales increased simultaneously. A new product's time to market, in this connection, has been evidently shortened. For instance, the Multifocus System, a recently introduced model which adjusts to the level of background noise, was brought to the market 6 months earlier than the previous ones due to reforms in the product development methods. Oticon has certainly raised its competitive position. It is all credited to its Metamorphosis.

Now, then, how do Metamorphosis and BPR essentially differ ? What corporate culture can be seen in the Metamorphosis ?

Let us next address these matters respectively. As N. Bjorn-Andersen and J. A. Turner put it, the basic difference between Metamorphosis and BPR is recognized in the following five dimensions.

1 Holistic vision
2 Focus on employees rather than business processes
3 Commitment
4 Participative rather than external driven approach
5 Culture

Holistic vision

All the authors on BPR assert that change has to be driven by a vision. What basically matters here, however, is who creates the vision and what it is all about. The BPR authors do not explicitly state the above matters, but only mention that a vision follows after a business process to be redesigned is found out.

The vision at Oticon was distinctly different ; it was a drastic statement of what the firm would like to be. Lars Kolind formulated it as follows : 'Be the No.1 hearing aid company by 1997'. (Ibid. P 10) The vision ought to be over and above men's wishes. It has to be a goal. To reach that goal, one needs to find out a coherent set of strategies.

In preparing strategies at Oticon, all the premises concerning the firm were put in question and all the traditional ways of business were rethought over and again. As a result, they came up with the following : reconceptualizing of the products, a totally new organizational structure, new job structure, new reward and incentive structure, new control structure, new office layout, new technology, a new firm ownership arrangement, and recognition that human resources are the most significant asset of the firm.

In the new control structure among the above, the way of self-control was adopted in place of its conventional supervision by the middle management. The firm stressed self-reliance among workers. In the new ownership arrangement, next, the greater part of ownership turned out to be held by the management and workers. It is characteristic of egalitarianism. The firm's acknowledgment, in addition, that human resources are the most important asset, obviously expresses the dignity of an individual.

Thus, Oticon's vision is very much holistic in nature including self-reliance, egalitarianism and an individual's dignity as an integral part of it which certainly represent Oticon's corporate culture.

Focus on employees rather than business processes

Focusing exclusively on business processes is in common among all BPR thoughts. To concentrate on business processes, excluding all the other factors that have influence over workers' behavior, tends not to promote changes but to maintain things as they are. Redesigning focused only on business processes leads to the facilitation of effectiveness to some extent at the sacrifice of innovation, flexibility, and other vital competitive elements.

At Oticon, the focus was not on business processes, but on the enhancement of motivation among individual employees. What was expected is that if barriers set before the workers were removed, and they were provided with advanced tools conducive to productivity in accordance with new skills, they would do well as individuals, perform consistently with the interests of the company, and would have a better quality of working life.

Commitment

For change to be successfully implemented along the lines set by a firm, workers have to firmly commit themselves to it. Their commitment, furthermore, needs to be motivated in affirmative and positive a manner.

At Oticon, employees are given stocks of the company every year. As of 1991, their share was 6 percent of the total ownership, but it is intended to be raised up to 25 percent in the future.

The other policy, to help motivate the workers to be committed to change, was to promote the 'fish-bowl' effect. Kars Kolind used stories about the re-invention of Oticon in the media to create a positive and desirable image of the firm. The stories were recounted many times as a fairy tale in the newspapers and other media in Denmark and overseas. As a result, the workers at Oticon attracted a good deal of public attention. It was increasingly difficult for them, therefore, to view their company negatively. They grew to view and think of things much more objectively. The fish-bowl effect really became in force. It represents openness and fairness which are also characteristic of the culture of Oticon.

Participative rather than external driven approach

BPR argues that worker participation is good when a firm goes through slow change, but not appropriate if it is faced with abrupt change. That is why BPR takes a top-down and an expert-led approach.

At Oticon, to the contrary, they followed the participative process. The change process was neither limited to a few managers nor led by outside consultants. Everyone was informed and involved in implementing the change. The greater part of that change, indeed, was undertaken and executed by workers themselves. Here is a way of thinking that one is a leading actor, which is another attribute of Oticon's culture. It is certain that the process was driven by the vision of Lars Kolind. His leadership was charismatic in nature, but it was a genuinely open process.

Culture

Such a frame-breaking change as occurred at Oticon needs egalitarian culture since it requires much of employees.

> The old Oticon was elitist. As an example, there were five classes of company cars depending on a person's managerial level. When Kolind joined the company, he was offered a royal-blue Jaguar XJ Sovereign 6.2, with leather seats and mahogany-panels, which had been driven by the former CEO. He thanked them and said that his old Saab would be good enough. It did not take long before the standard tier of company cars had adjusted itself. It is clear that Kolind is keen to have as little distance as possible between the top and bottom of the firm. He might even argue that there is no bottom at all. (Ibid. P 12)

At Oticon, egalitarianism also shows itself in the way that they think and address information technology. In BPR, IT is an essential part of rethought even if it is not the primary driving force. IT was never the starting point, however, in preparing the plan for organizational change at Oticon. Although he vaguely thought what IT could do, Kolind formed his vision without its detailed analysis. It is not IT but men and women that are given the first priority. IT is to serve people. Thus, IT turned out to serve the workers by providing information whenever and wherever they need. There is no thought of controlling people by IT. People first, and IT to follow and serve them. That is the way of thinking characteristic of Oticon.

As have been seen, the Metamorphosis and BPR are essentially different, which is particularly evident as viewed from Oticon's corporate culture. Oticon is typical of a metamorphosed company. It deserves the title of a 21 century company since there is thorough egalitarianism in its modes of viewing and ways of thinking. Without its egalitarianism, the crux of its corporate culture, Oticon's metamorphosis could not have been successfully achieved.

Corporate culture changes. Oticon's culture may change in time as others do. With the firm's dynamic state, therefore, people at Oticon would be recommended to observe continually how its structure of competitiveness, in which their culture is duly reflected, may change. It is the firm's competitiveness structure, in the final analysis, that determines its performance.

14 The leading firm in the 21st century

What is most characteristic of leading firms in the 21st century ?   In other words, what are the things indispensable for a firm to be viable in the 21st century ? To be viable, a firm should fit the Three-Layer Structure of Enterprise Competitiveness and have a corresponding healthy corporate culture.   We shall, however, develop our argument further on that point. What are the vital elements needed for a firm in such an unknown time and space as the 21st century ?   The author thinks that they are entrepreneurship and innovation, in particular, out of those elements in the Competitiveness Structure. The following is, therefore, exclusively focused on these two elements.

Now, it is often said that a big corporation lacks entrepreneurship and innovation. It sounds plausible in a way since most new and remarkable innovations in this century have not been created by big corporations.

> The railroads did not spawn the automobile or the truck ; they did not even try. And though the automobile companies did try (Ford and General Motors both pioneered in aviation and aerospace), all of today's large aircraft and aviation companies have evolved out of separate new ventures. Similarly, today's giants of the pharmaceutical industry are, in the main, companies that were small or nonexistent fifty years ago when the first modern drugs were developed. Every one of the giants of the electrical industry...General Electric, Westinghouse, and RCA in the United States ; Siemens and Philips on the Continent ; Toshiba in Japan...rushed into computers in the 1950s. Not one was successful. The field is dominated by IBM, a company that was barely middle-sized and most definitely not high-tech forty years ago. (Peter F. Drucker, 1993 P 147)

It is not, however, necessarily true that big firms are not entrepreneurial or innovative. This is a misunderstanding because there have been many exceptions to that assertion, and in fact there are quite a few large and yet innovative organizations.

> In the United States, there is Johnson & Johnson in hygiene and health care, and 3M in highly engineered products for both industrial and consumer markets. Citibank, America's and the world's largest non-governmental financial institution, well over a century old, has been a major innovator in many areas of banking and finance. In Germany, Hoechst...one of the world's largest chemical companies, and more than 125 years old by now ... has become a successful innovator in the pharmaceutical industry. In Sweden, ASEA, founded in 1884 and for the last sixty or seventy years a very big company, is a true innovator in both long-distance transmission of electrical power and robotics for factory automation. (Ibid. PP 147-148)

Secondly, it is not right to argue that bigness does harm to entrepreneurship and innovation. When people talk of a big-sized firm, they often refer to bureaucracy and conservatism. It is certain that such traits exist in big companies. However, it is to be noted that other traits are in existence as well in those firms. What mostly hinders entrepreneurship and innovation is not the size of a firm, but its existing operation, in particular, its successful operation.

What is to be attentive, therefore, is a firm's present business, whether it is a small company or a large one. The present business always requires the highest priority in the allocation of resources. On the other hand, innovators usually start a new effort as small and simple. Thus, it needs a special endeavor to get entrepreneurial and innovative things done well. Within a firm, people tend to allocate resources largely among the existing operations, and provide small or minimal ones to things new or new ventures. If a firm does not invest in new and innovative things, it will age and deteriorate with time. Yet, in a period of rapid change like the present, its deterioration is sure to be very fast. Once a company is accustomed to looking back, it has difficulty turning around to look forward.

The more successful a firm's present operation, the longer the delayed to become entrepreneurial and innovative. To look for entrepreneurship and innovation incessantly, therefore, demands exceeding efforts. But there are, in fact, a number of companies that have been successful in their endeavors to be entrepreneurial and innovative.

We shall, thus, take up and explain what is essentially needed for such a success while referring to cases of success and failure.

What is necessary to render a firm receptive to innovation ? At first, there must be an understanding in the organization that innovation is more attractive and of greater value than to hold on to convention. That is, an understanding is to prevail throughout the organization that innovation is the best means to maintain and perpetuate a firm and most conducive to the welfare of its constituent people. There needs a climate where Newness and Youngness (US culture), and Musubi and Yomigaeri (Japanese culture) can be active on the scene. To build that climate, the first thing to do is to work out a policy or develop a system that aged, obsolete and unproductive things are to be discarded. That is the right way to maintain the health of an organization. Whatever organism it is, indeed, it does harm to itself unless it throws away its waste. Therefore, a policy or system of discarding things harmful to advancement is essential if a firm is to go on to innovate.

Innovation demands a great effort. It requires hard work of talented people. Yet, such talents are very limited and scarce in any organization. But, when the constituents of an organization come to understand that things dead are to be buried and those of innovation are to be taken up and engaged in, their endeavors will be rewarded. To render an organization innovative, the firm must free its talent to challenge innovation, while its financial resources have to be directed toward innovation. It is necessary, furthermore, not to hold on to the success of the past and, therefore, it is preferable to abandon it. When a firm has established a basic and firm policy or system of discarding the past, it is then expected that people look for things new and facilitate entrepreneurship in their behavior.

The second thing needed to encourage creating an innovative climate is that people understand that the present products, services, markets and others have limited health and life expectancies. In other words, it is of significance that people understand how much an existing business requires innovation, in what areas and what time frame.

The best and simplest approach to this was developed by Michael J. Kami as a member of the Entrepreneurship Seminar at the New York University Graduate Business School in the 1950s. Kami first applied his approach to IBM, where he served as head of business planning ; and then, in the early 1960s, to Xerox, where he served for several years in a similar capacity.

In this approach a company lists each of its products or services, but also the markets each serves and the distributive channels it uses, in order to estimate their position on the product life cycle. How much longer will it still maintain itself in the marketplace ? How soon can it be expected to age and decline...and how fast ? When will it become obsolescent ? This enables the company to estimate where it would be if it confined itself to managing to the best of its ability what already exists.

And this then shows the gap between what can be expected realistically, and what a company still needs to do to achieve its objectives, whether in sales, in market standing, or in profitability. The gap is the minimum that must be filled if the company is not to go downhill. In fact, the gap has to be filled or the company will soon start to die. The entrepreneurial achievement must be large enough to fill the gap, and timely enough to fill it before the old becomes obsolescent. (Ibid. PP 153-154)

With the approach above, it becomes apparent how it is necessary to allocate resources, such as money and people, to the pursuit of innovation. Among other things, finally, a firm's leader has to be a person who perceives innovation as the healthy, normal and necessary course of action if the firm is truly to attain and maintain an entrepreneurial climate. Future-Orientedness of a business leader and his mind of Musubi is the key to success.

Entrepreneurial practices

For a firm to be entrepreneurial, its management practices are to be duly set up. In a firm trying to create the receptivity to entrepreneurship, special regard is given to how business reports and meetings are to be held effectively. Typically, there are two types of meetings on operating results in such a firm. That is, one is concerned with the problems of operations and the other with the opportunities in dealing with the problems.

One medium-sized supplier of health-care products to physicians and hospitals, a company that has gained leadership in a number of new and promising fields, holds an 'operations meeting' the second and the last Monday of each month. The first meeting is devoted to problems...to all the things which, in the last month, have done less well than expected or are still doing less well than expected six months later. This meeting does not differ one whit from any other operating meeting. But the second meeting...the one on the last Monday...discusses the areas where the company is doing better than expected : the sales of a given product that have grown faster than projected, or the orders for a new product that are coming in from markets for which it was not designed. The top management of the company (which has grown ten-fold in twenty years) believes that its success is primarily the result of building this opportunity focus into its monthly management meetings. 'The opportunities we spot it there,' the chief executive officer has said many times, 'are not nearly as important as the entrepreneurial attitude which the habit of looking for opportunities creates throughout the entire management group.' This company follows a second practice to generate an entrepreneurial spirit throughout its entire management group. Every six months it holds a two-day management meeting for all executives in charge of divisions, markets, and major product lines...a group of about forty or fifty people. The first morning is set aside for reports to the entire group from three or four executives whose units have done exceptionally well as entrepreneurs and innovators during the past year. They are expected to report on what explains their success : 'What did we do that turned out to be successful ?' 'How did we find the opportunity ?' 'What have we learned, and what entrepreneurial and innovative plans do we have in hand now ?' (Ibid. PP 156-157)

What is meaningful here is not the contents of reports presented, but whatever positive influence is exerted to the attitudes and values of management people while talking about such opportunities. It is stressed time and again how many new ideas managers have after those sessions.

Next, there is an informal meeting which companies, particularly, large ones regard as a significant practice. In such an informal meeting, it is usually the case that one member of the top management group sits down with junior people from research, engineering, manufacturing, marketing and others in the organization.

The senior opens the session by saying : 'I'm not here to make a speech or to tell you anything, I'm here to listen. I want to hear from you what your aspirations are, but above all, where you see opportunities for this company and where you see threats. And what are your ideas for us to try to do new things, develop new products, design new ways of reaching the market ? What questions do you have about the company, its policies, its direction .... its position in the industry, in technology, in the marketplace ?' (Ibid. P 157)

The meeting above mentioned could provide the juniors a good opportunity for upward communication while they come to understand what the top management are concerned with. Such a meeting is informal, literally, and free in its atmosphere so that it would help prepare an arena for the attribute of Taking Things Easy in the US culture and those of Kotodama and Matsuri in the Japanese culture to be in full action. It would be the right place for an entrepreneurial vision to be diffused.

Measurement of entrepreneurial performance

For a firm's performance to be really entrepreneurial, there needs to be a procedure or a system to see if innovative projects have been carried out and lived up to top management expectations. In other words, measurement is to be conducted periodically between the feedback results of each project and the expectations at the start.

> One of the most successful of the world's major banks attributes its achievements to the feedback it builds into all new efforts, whether it is going into a new market such as South Korea, into equipment leasing, or into issuing credit cards. By building feedback from results to expectations for all new endeavors, the bank and its top management have also learned what they can expect from new ventures : How soon a new effort can be expected to produce results and when it should be supported by greater efforts and greater resources. (Ibid. P 159)

In addition to the feedback measurement above, developing a systematic review of innovative efforts and having periodic meetings about such reviews is especially important.

> The top management people at one of the world's largest and most successful pharmaceutical companies sit down once a year to review its innovative efforts. First, they review every new drug development, asking : 'Is this development going in the right direction and at the right speed ? Is it leading to something we want to put into our own line, or is it going to be something that won't fit our markets so we'd better license it to another pharmaceutical manufacturer ? Or ought we perhaps abandon it ?' And then the same people look at all the other innovative efforts, especially in marketing, asking exactly the same questions. Finally, they review, equally carefully, the innovative performance of their major competitors. In terms of its research budget and its total expenditures for innovation, this company ranks only in the middle level. Its record as an innovator and entrepreneur is, however, outstanding. (Ibid. P 160)

149

What is the most significant thing in measuring entrepreneurial performance ? No doubt, it is leadership. Unless a firm's leader is entrepreneurial or innovative, the measurement of performance would only be a ritual and not instrumental at all in helping to create new things. To put it another way, the performance measurement is also the acid test of the leader's Integrity and Fairness or his Akaki-Kokoro.

Structure of organization

Innovation is created by people. They work, on the other hand, within a structure of organization. Accordingly, one has to devise an organization' structure that helps them to be entrepreneurial. Basically, it is a rule to organize things entrepreneurial and separate new areas from the existing and old organization. One reason is that an existing business always requires people to focus on immediate issues. Even if they are placed in charge of a new venture, they are likely to postpone their activities necessary for that until it is too late. For this reason, whatever new venture in an organization needs to be assigned to someone in the top management group. Innovative efforts are, thus, to be directly reported to that senior person in charge. If that rule is neglected, it would cause a sizable cost.

> The company had the basic patents on machine tools for automated mass production. It had excellent engineering, an excellent reputation, and first-rate manufacturing. Everyone in the early years of factory automation...around 1975...expected it to emerge as the leader. Ten years later it had dropped out of the race entirely. The company had placed the unit charged with the development of machine tools for automated production three or four levels down in the organization, and had it report to people charged with designing, making, and selling the company's traditional machine-tool lines. These people were supportive ; in fact, the work on robotics had been mainly their idea. But they were far too busy defending their traditional lines against a lot of new competitors such as the Japanese, redesigning them to fit new specifications, demonstrating, marketing, financing, and servicing them. Whenever the people in charge of the 'infant' went to their bosses for a decision, they were told, 'I have no time now, come back next week.' Robotics were, after all, only a promise ; the existing machine-tool lines produced millions of dollars each year. (Ibid. P 163)

On the other hand, what if a firm does not make the above error and observes the rule ?

The best known practitioners of this approach are three American companies : Procter & Gamble, the soap, detergent, edible oil, and food producer...a very large and aggressively entrepreneurial company ; Johnson & Johnson, the hygiene and health-care supplier ; 3M, a major manufacturer of industrial and consumer products. These three companies differ in the details of practice but essentially all three have the same policy. They set up the new venture as a separate business from the beginning and put a project manager in charge. The project manager remains in charge until the project is either abandoned or has achieved its objective and become a full-fledged business. And until then, the project manager can mobilize all the skills as they are needed...research, manufacturing, finance, marketing...and put them to work on the project team. (Ibid. PP 163-164)

A venture in the organization requires a man who has full time for it, pays necessary attention to it, tries to understand where problems are in executing it and makes the crucial decisions. He should also be, preferably, among the top management group.

Another reason that a new innovative effort is best set up separate from the old is that it is to be independent of the measurement of a general return on investment. We can cite a major chemical company's case in that regard.

Everybody knew that one of its central divisions had to produce new materials to stay in business. The plans for these materials were there, the scientific work had been done...but nothing happened. Year after year there was another excuse. Finally, the division's general manager spoke up at a review meeting, 'My management group and I are compensated primarily on the basis of return-on-investment. The moment we spend money on developing the new materials, our return will go down by half at least four years. Even if I am still here in four years time when we should show the first returns on these investments...and I doubt that the company will put up with me that long if profits are that much lower...I'm taking bread out of the mouths of all my associates in the meantime. Is it reasonable to expect us to do this ?' The formula was changed and the developmental expenses for the new project were taken out of the return-on-investment figures. Within eighteen months the new materials were on the market. Two years later they had given the division leadership in its field which it has retained to this day. Four years later the division doubled its profits. (Ibid. P 165)

In that context, there is the matter of how to compensate and reward people engaged in new ventures. It is natural that they should be treated with rewards and benefits appropriate to their endeavors. In reality, it is the right way to provide them with the same compensation and benefits that they receive in their existing work at the time of launching the new venture. Then, the top management had better promise them that they can gain a reward of success if the new venture turns out to be successful. That kind of promise would be effective in drawing out people's Individualism or their Yaoyorozu-No-Kami.

One method that 3M and Johnson & Johnson use effectively is to promise that the person who successfully develops a new product, a new market, or a new service and then builds a business on it will become the head of that business : general manager, vice-president, or division president, with the rank, compensation, bonuses, and stock options appropriate to the level. This can be a sizable reward, and yet it does not commit the company to anything except in case of success. Another method...and which one is preferable will depend largely on the tax laws at the time...is to give the people who take on the new development a share in future profits. The venture might, for instance, be treated as if it were a separate company in which the entrepreneurial managers in charge have a stake, say 25 percent. When the venture reaches maturity, they are bought out at a pre-set formula based on sales and profits. (Ibid. PP 165-166)

On the other hand, the idea is also important that the top management shares the risk accompanied with a new venture. That is, it is considered to be sensible to leave an opportunity for people participating in a new venture to return to their old jobs. One should not penalize people for trying if they fail. In other words, they ought to be all the time provided opportunities of Yomigaeri. Innovative efforts are to be carried out in an environment that people can work with Future-Orientedness.

Finally, an organization for entrepreneurship is to be held responsible for the venture concerned, and operated as a totally separate entity.

The earliest example of this was set up more than one hundred years ago, in 1872, by Hefner-Alteneck, the first college-trained engineer hired by a manufacturing company anywhere, the German Siemens Company. Hefner started the first 'research lab' in industry. Its members were charged with inventing new and different products and processes. But they were also responsible for identifying new and different end uses and new and different markets. And they not only did the technical work ; they were responsible for development of the manufacturing process, for the introduction of the new product into the marketplace, and for its profitability. Fifty years later, in the 1920s, the American DuPont Company independently set up a similar unit and called it a Development Department. This department gathers innovative ideas from all over the company, studies them, thinks them through, analyzes them. Then it proposes to top management which ones should be tackled as major innovative projects. From the beginning, it brings to bear on the innovation all the resources needed : research, development, manufacturing, marketing, finance, and so on. It is in charge until the new product or service has been on the market for a few years. (Ibid. P 168)

To be certain, in that context, a top manager's personality and attitudes are a major element in maintaining an entrepreneurial and innovative organization. It does not, however, tell the whole story. To repeat, as we have stated so far, there must be the right and appropriate policies and practices built into the organization.

In the few short-lived cases I know of, the companies were built and still run by the founder. Even then, when it gets to be successful the company soon ceases to be entrepreneurial unless it adopts the policies and practices of entrepreneurial management. The reason why top management personalities and attitudes do not suffice in any but the very young or very small business is, of course, that even a medium-sized enterprise is a pretty large organization. It requires a good many people who know what they are supposed to do, want to do it, are motivated toward doing it, and are supplied with both the tools and continuous reaffirmation. Otherwise there is only lip service ; entrepreneurship soon becomes confined to the CEO's speeches. And I know of no business that continued to remain entrepreneurial beyond the founder's departure, unless the founder had built into the organization the policies and practices of entrepreneurial management. If these are lacking, the business becomes timid and backward-looking within a few years at the very latest. And these companies do not even realize, as a rule, that they have lost their essential quality, the one element that had made them stand out, until it is perhaps too late. For this realization one needs a measurement of entrepreneurial performance. (Ibid. P 169)

153

Things to be avoided

We have so far explained the things significant and essential in encouraging entrepreneurship and innovation in the organization. Now, let us look at the other side to see what is to be avoided in pursuing entrepreneurship and innovation from being hindered. First, one ought not to mix entrepreneurial units with managerial ones. The entrepreneurial thing is not to be included in the managerial practice. That is, innovation is not to be put into the work area of people charged with existing businesses.

> In the last ten or fifteen years a great many large American companies have tried to go into joint ventures with entrepreneurs. Not one of these attempts has succeeded ; the entrepreneurs found themselves stymied by policies, by basic rules, by a 'climate' they felt was bureaucratic, stodgy, reactionary. But at the same time their partners, the people from the big company, could not figure out what the entrepreneurs were trying to do and thought them undisciplined, wild, visionary. (Ibid. P 174)

Generally speaking, a big firm will succeed in a new venture only if it uses its own people. The firm will succeed if it uses people who knows it well, who it can trust, and puts people in innovative areas who can work as good partners. In other words, a successful firm has entrepreneurial climate and entrepreneurial practices in its own way.

A company is a gathering of people. It is needed, first and foremost, that people recognize each other as individuals and esteem their personalities respectively, which would help prepare a right place for Individualism and Yaoyorozu-No-Kami to be duly active.

The next thing to avoid is to try to carry out an entrepreneurial business through acquisitions. Acquisitions do not work well unless a firm puts necessary and capable talents of its own into its acquired company in quite a short time. Managers accompanied with an acquired company, mostly, will not remain long. If a firm wishes a business to be innovative and to have a good chance to succeed, it has to build an entrepreneurial management in its organization. Unless the whole of a firm is innovative and entrepreneurial, indeed, whatever new efforts they make would be unsuccessful in the end. It is all the people of a firm that are in stake with entrepreneurship and innovation.

Summary

A fundamental objective, for a firm living generation after generation, is to make and maintain a healthy organization and to follow the Three-Layer Structure of Enterprise Competitiveness. This is vital for the leading firms in the 21st century. Yet, out of the competitiveness elements in an organization, the elements of entrepreneurship and innovation are particularly important. How to nurture, develop and maintain those elements is the key to success in the coming century.

Epilogue

Enterprise competitiveness is structurally composed of three layers. The first layer is the Enterprise Logistics, comprising Enterprise ethos, Enhancement of initiative, Provision of norms, Preparation of investment conditions, Enterprise ethics and Education. It is the outermost layer, surrounding the second and the third layers. The second layer is the Enterprise Economic Base, including Infrastructure, Environment improvement and conservation, and Diffusion of new ideas, planning and others. This is the layer that supports the arena for actors, i.e., the Management System. The third layer is, then, the Management System in which Effectiveness, Tense balance between effectiveness and ethics, and Ethics are comprised. It rests at the core of the Three-Layer Structure and at the center of enterprise competitiveness. Thus, the three-layer structure above forms the competitiveness of an enterprise.

Enterprise competitiveness is the competitiveness of a company. It is formed and supported by its constituent people. The constituents have, in turn, cultural attributes characteristic of their country reflected in their modes of viewing things, ways of thinking and state of being. On the other hand, corporate culture is the personality of a firm. It is yet cultural factors ascribed to people of a firm that form its personality. The combination and degree of strength each of those attributes differ from one company to another. That difference represents, in reality, a company's corporate culture, i.e., its personality.

Quite recently, at the end of the 1970s, corporate culture became an area of study in the field of business administration. There are now three theories on corporate culture, namely, Theory I. Strong cultures, Theory II. Strategically appropriate cultures, and Theory III. Adaptive cultures. The author's view on corporate culture and performance does not belong to any of the above theories.

In his view, there is, generally, good cultural content suited to every condition. That content is healthy, adaptive to change, and includes

156

things of value to be preserved. Secondly, it is firmly associated with the elements of the competitiveness structure. That is, a culture that fits in well with the Three-Layer Structure of Enterprise Competitiveness produces a superior performance in the long run. The author names that view the 'Theory IV'.

We have taken up several examples of corporate culture to explain it in details. The first example cited is Ohmi Merchants in the Tokugawa times. In their way of business, there is recognized a solid competitiveness structure. Due to its solidness, most of their businesses have been kept on to this day in an unbroken succession. We can also see the cultural attributes of theirs that are highly adaptive to that structure of competitiveness. Those attributes include Akaki-Kokoro, Yaoyorozu-No-Kami, Musubi, Kotodama, Kanjyo, Many Deities as One Deity, One Deity as Many Deities, and Hajio-Shiru-Kokoro. In other words, the modes of viewing, the ways of thinking and state of being of Ohmi Merchants are rightfully and collectively reflected in the competitiveness structure, which forms the personality of Ohmi Merchants, i.e., Ohmi Merchants' culture in its own way.

The second is Hewlett-Packard chosen as an example of today's healthy corporate culture. What is known as the HP way today originates in a philosophy fundamental to business and ways of operations developed by its founders, i.e., Bill Hewlett, Dave Packard and their colleagues. The crux of the HP way lies in the way of thinking that a firm is to serve everyone who has a stake in the business with integrity and fairness. Its adaptability to changes was tested in the 1970s and the 1980s. The result was that they went through a bitter and adverse environment successfully. In 1992, furthermore, they incontrovertibly plowed through the economic downturn again with its culture intact although they had to address difficult decisions on downsizing. It is testified by the study on Hewlett-Packard UK by P. McGovern and V. Hope-Hailey. Hewlett-Packard is a typical example of firms with culture highly adaptive to the Three-Layer Structure of Enterprise Competitiveness.

The third is Xerox selected as an example of unhealthy corporate culture. Xerox's inappropriateness to the Three-Layer Structure of Enterprise Competitiveness is all the more apparent as viewed from the US culture perspective. In Xerox during the 1970s, an atmosphere did not exist that allowed people to grapple with any situation without hesitation and without worrying about failure. That was no place for Youngness, Newness and Future-Orientedness, three attributes of the US culture, to live with. Individualism was not recognized in that there is no view that every member is a leading actor ; in that the personnel lose pride and confidence in upholding their enterprise's competitiveness as well as a sense of representing their enterprise. Next, it is opposed to Diligence that the company decided to purchase a firm only to acquire market share. It is, furthermore, indicative of loss of the attribute of Taking Things Easy that the decision-making was centralized ; that the managers were only concerned with figures, and so not a good communicator to their staff. Finally, it represents the management's being little conscious of Competition that their interest in stockholders and costs weakened ; and that they were little conscious of effectiveness. Taken together, Xerox in the 1970s was typical of a firm with unhealthy culture which is inappropriate to the Three-Layer Structure of Enterprise Competitiveness.

The fourth example cited is Nissan as a firm that has attempted a turnaround from its unhealthy culture. To turn from its bureaucratic structure of organization, several innovative changes have been implemented since Yutaka Kume was appointed president in 1985. The first visible and innovative change appeared in the development of the Silvia, a new model car. The Silvia project was wholly committed to young employees. It represents a break from tradition in Nissan's centralized bureaucracy in that the decision-making was left to young employees. Along with the project of Silvia, there was the introduction of Simultaneous engineering by which Diffusion of new ideas, planning and others was promoted. A flex time system was also introduced which is conducive to Enhancement of initiative in that it helps to add to pride and confidence in employees' own work. In implementing these changes, there are recognized such attributes of Japanese culture as Yomigaeri, Musubi, Kotodama, Yaoyorozu-No-Kami and others being active.

The fifth example shown is the Confucianist Company, an unhealthy corporate culture in Japan. The company has four main characteristics in its modes of viewing things, ways of thinking and state of being. The first characteristic is its paying a great regard to social stratum. The second is a rule-by-virtue principle. The third is classicism and the fourth is family-circle homogeneity. These characteristics are utterly inappropriate to the Three-Layer Structure of Enterprise Competitiveness. Confucianism is not the mainstream of Japanese culture. Its remnant, however, still remains. It exercises an adverse effect on the competitiveness of a firm and drives its performance literally down. Ei Muramatsu calls that adverse effect the 'Poison of Confucianism'. Business leaders would be recommended to find, take away, and eradicate that poison before it gets deep inside the organization and does harm to it.

Corporate culture changes. It changes if there occurs some transformation in the constituents' modes of viewing, ways of thinking and state of being. If it is a healthy transformation, it is to be encouraged. If not, it is to be stopped and turned around the right way. Healthiness of a firm's culture is measured by the degree of its adaptability to the Three-Layer Structure of Enterprise Competitiveness. Accordingly, business leaders had better keep in mind the significant attributes of corporate culture which are most appropriate to the Competitiveness Structure. In Chapter 12, Section 1 in this context, we have described the representative attributes of healthy corporate culture.

Finally, we have addressed the case of Oticon, a Danish concern and the conditions indispensable and essential for the leading firm in the 21st century. Many years have past since the business process redesign or reengineering was widely propagated as a means to enhance corporate performance. Few firms that employed it, however, have succeeded in improving their performance. In that context, the study of Oticon by Niels Bjorn-Andersen and Jon A.Turner is truly reflective and insightful. They argue that it is Metamorphosis that helps heighten corporate performance, while duly pointing out the defects ascribed to the thought of BPR. The Metamorphosis means, in our words, to phenomenally raise an organization's adaptability to the Three-Layer Structure of Enterprise Competitiveness. Through the Metamorphosis, i.e., a frame-breaking, Oticon made a complete breakaway from its conventional practices. The firm deserves the title of a 21 century company since there is thorough egalitarianism in their modes of viewing and ways of thinking. Without its egalitarianism, the crux of its corporate culture, Oticon's metamorphosis could not have been successfully achieved. Next, we have come up with the essential elements needed for the leading a firm in the 21st century. Entrepreneurship and innovation are certain to be the most indispensable ingredients for the years to come since they are not only significant practices but to be naturally and positively interwined with good and healthy corporate culture.

A company is a living being. It has the personality of its own. How does such a living being with its own personality build up competitiveness ? Here is a linkage between corporate culture and competitiveness. It is the key to uncover the relationship between corporate culture and performance.

Bibliography

Benedict, Ruth. (1954), *The Chrysanthemum and the Sword*, Charles E. Tuttle Co., Inc. : Tokyo.

Bjorn-Andersen, Niels and Turner, Jon A. (1995), *Creating The 21 Century Organization : The Metamorphosis of Oticon*, Leonard N. Stern School of Business: New York University.

Council on Competitiveness. (1991) *Gaining New Ground, Technology Priorities for America's Future*, Council on Competitiveness : Washington D. C.

Deal, Terry E. and Kennedy, Allan A. (1982), *Corporate Cultures*, Addison-Wesley : Reading, Mass.

Drucker, Peter F. (1993), *Innovation and Entrepreneurship*, Harper Business : New York.

Ferraro, Gary P. (1990), *The Cultural Dimension of International Business*, Prentice Hall Inc. : New York.

Hasegawa, Toshiaki. (1991), *Kyoso Shakai America* [The Competitive Society America], Chuo Koron-sha : Tokyo.

Higuchi, Kiyoyuki. (1988), *Umeboshi to Nihon-tau* [Pickled Japanese Apricot and Japanese Sword], Shoden-sha : Tokyo.

Kato, Hidetoshi. (1968), *Hikaku Bunka eno Shikaku* [A Viewpoint of Comparative Study on Culture], Chuo Koron-sha : Tokyo.

Kiplinger, A. H. and Kiplinger, K. A. (1989), *America in the Global '90 s*, Kiplinger Books : Washington D. C.

Kotter, John P. and Heskett, James L. (1992), *Corporate Culture and Performance*, The Free Press : New York.

Laubacher, Robert J., Malone, Thomas W. and the MIT Scenario Working Group. (1997), *Two Scenario for 21st Century Organizations*, Sloan School of Management : MIT.

McGovern, Patrick G. and Hope-Hailey, Veronica. (1996), *Inside Hewlett-Packard : Corporate culture and bureaucratic control*, Center for Organizational Research, London Business School : UK.

Muramatsu, Ei. (1994), *Jyukyo no Doku* [Poison of Confucianism], PHP Kenkyu-jyo : Tokyo.

Naisbitt, John and Aburdene, Patricia. (1986), *Re-inventing the Corporation*, Warner Books : New York.

Nakane, Chie. (1984), *Japanese Society*, Charles E. Tuttle Co., Inc. : Tokyo.

Ogura, Eiichiro. (1990), *Ohmi Shonin no Keifu* [History of Ohmi Merchants], Shakai Shiso-sha : Tokyo.

Okumura, H., Sasako, K., Sataka, M. and Others. (1994), *Kigyo Tanken* [Exploration of Corporations], Shakai-Shiso-Sha : Tokyo.

Ouchi, William. (1981), *Theory Z*, Addison-Wesley : Reading, Mass.

Pascale, Richard T. and Athos, Anthony G. (1981), *The Art of Japanese Management*, Simon & Schuster : New York.

Peters, Tom and Waterman, Robert H. Jr. (1995), *In Search of Excellence*, Harper Collins Publisher : New York.

Porter, Michael. (1989), *The Competitive Advantage of Nations*, The Macmillan Press Ltd. : London.

Shiba, Ryotaro. (1989), *America Subyo* [Rough Sketch of America], Shincho-sha : Tokyo.

Shibata, Minoru. (1962), *Jinbutsu Sosho Ishida Baigan* [Profile of Baigan Ishida], Yoshikawa Kobunkan : Tokyo.

Shibata, Minoru et al. (1956), *Ishida Baigan Zenshu* [A Series of Baigan Ishida's], Meirin-sha : Tokyo.

Starr, M. K. (1988), *Global Competitiveness*, W.W. Norton & Co. : New York.

Suzuki, Takao. (1973), *Kotoba to Bunka* [Language and Culture], Iwanami Shoten : Tokyo.

Yamashita, Hideo. (1996), *Competitiveness and the Kami Way*, Ashgate Publishing Ltd. : Aldershot, U.K.

For Product Safety Concerns and Information please contact our EU
representative GPSR@taylorandfrancis.com Taylor & Francis Verlag GmbH,
Kaufingerstraße 24, 80331 München, Germany

Printed and bound by CPI Group (UK) Ltd, Croydon, CR0 4YY
08/05/2025
01864410-0002